Connected Cognitive Coaching

A MODEL FOR LEADERSHIP HEALTH AND WELLNESS COACHES

PAT A. TAMAKLOE, Ph.D.

CONNECTED COGNITIVE COACHING:
A Model for Leadership Health and Wellness Coaches

Copyright © 2025 Pat A. Tamakloe, Ph.D.

ISBN (Paperback): 979-8-89672-018-8
ISBN (Hardback): 979-8-89672-019-5
ISBN (Ebook): 979-8-89672-020-1

Printed in the United States of America.

PROMINENT
BOOKS

5830 E 2nd St, Ste 7000 #9983
Casper, WY 82609
USA

DEDICATION

To the Certified Organizational Change Agents (COCAs) of Global Reach Leadership Institute Inc. and the network of coaches in the Connected Cognitive Coaching Consortium International (C4I) group, for dedicating your lives to leadership-behavior transformation across the globe, using uniquely tailored strategies to attain results and for allowing me to earn the permission to lead you in fulfilling your purpose.

CONTENTS

ACKNOWLEDGMENTS

Firstly, I want to thank God, my family, and my fellow thought leaders of the Connected Cognitive Coaching Consortium International (C4I) for their commitment to testing this model. Their critiques were invaluable in enabling the development of this book.

Nature would fail me if I began to name those who influenced this writing. Therefore, I humbly acknowledge anyone who knows he or she added value to me on this journey to finish this work. Thank you for your love and support. Never forget to lead the change!

INTRODUCTION

I was at a crossroads in my career at almost twenty years of naval service, and I had several decisions to make quickly. That morning while in self-reflection, I sat on the bedroom floor with my head in my hands. I pressed my back firmly against the wall. My face was planted squarely in the palm of my hands, and my neck was hyperextended as I gazed and daydreamed. I was drained and was exhausted from the thoughts running through my mind. *What am I going to do at this juncture in my life? I am still young with several big dreams yet to accomplish*, I thought. *I cannot concentrate or make the best of what I do for a living because my mind is always racing at one hundred miles per hour. I don't enjoy what I do now as a profession. Therefore, I feel unfulfilled in my role as a leader. I am hung up on my true purpose, and it's time to move on to something that adds value to others. This is where my strength is. This is where I create impact—helping people overcome their past hurts and hang-ups. While talking to my last commanding officer, who was worth his eagle-collar devices, I realized I had impacted his life. I will succeed in my quest to change the world after all, impacting leaders, where feasible, across the globe.*

This was the conversation in my mind that fateful day when I decided to retire early from active duty as a commissioned naval officer and to transition into business to pursue my entrepreneurial dreams. You see, you will never be happy with yourself until you find yourself. By that, I mean fulfillment comes when you find something that consumes your time and effort without being compensated for it because you love doing it. Several leaders worldwide are stuck in pause regarding their careers, which don't define their true purpose in life. They are unfulfilled, unresolved, and unaccomplished where they are because they are in the wrong sphere of influence where they may be stressed, dysfunctional, tired or simply mentally, physically and socially unhealthy. There is no fun and impact in what they do. I was there. Just as I heard it said in the navy several times before, "If you stop having fun, it's time to go," I also heard, "If you do what you love, you'll never have to work a day in your life."

My time came sooner than most expected to fulfill my passionate drive. I had aspirations to do more than lead men and women into battle in defense of our national interests. Don't get me wrong; I am proud of every moment I served. It was not that I loved my naval service less but that I loved organizational-leadership transformation more. Helping both the young and old make a mental transition from their pasts, through their present, and toward where they desired to be was exactly what my heart desired. Yes, as Steve Jobs so eloquently said that those who are crazy enough to think they can change the world are actually the ones who do, I am committed to doing so in my circle of influence and intellect. I discovered my purpose later in life than I would have preferred. Today, I have counseled and coached several successful men and women to attain their leadership goals and objectives across organizations, especially in business organizations. I intend to continue doing so until I draw my last breath.

So what is this passionate drive? It's helping leaders find healthy habits and wellness practices to take care of their mental/spiritual, physical, and social health so that they can perform at their peak in any sphere of influence. It's leadership health and wellness, a term

I coined, which focuses on a leader's holistic, adequate functioning and productivity in all aspects of the leader's personal and professional being. The National Institute of Wellness defines wellness as a conscious, self-directed process involving several personal and professional attributes contributing to one's overall functioning[1].

Increasing research in emerging leadership theories such as health-oriented leadership models show that there is a growing need and demand for leaders to take good care of themselves so that their teams can also do the same to ultimately take care of their customers or clients. In one case, researchers determined in their study after conducting multiple regression study analyses, there was substantial evidence to suggest that a leader's enhanced self-care leads to their staff's increased engagement levels as well as their reduced exhaustion levels.[2] This notion of self-care for leaders must consequently become an integral part of any leader's coaching or leadership health to ensure their optimum performance and success.

For a moment, let's consider a paradigm of leadership success—mindfulness. Mindfulness has become a new buzzword across organizations. Yet few know of its impact and relationship to organizational leadership success. It is the same as the way one's health and wellness connect to one's success as an organizational leader. By that, I mean a leader's cognitive health and wellness, as wellness or health does not only pertain to eating our fruits and vegetables while we exercise regularly. It also involves having well-balanced mental

---

[1] NWI's Six Dimensions of Wellness, National Wellness Institute, accessed April 15, 2022, *https://nationalwellness.org/resources/six-dimensions-of-wellness/*

[2] Grimm, Luisa A., Georg F. Bauer, and Gregor J. Jenny. "Is the Health-Awareness of Leaders Related to the Working Conditions, Engagement, and Exhaustion in Their Teams? A Multi-Level Mediation Study." *BMC Public Health* 21, no. 1 (October 24, 2021). https://doi.org/10.1186/s12889-021-11985-1.

and social states for one's peak performance. Most leadership health and wellness coaching will enhance the leader's cognitive or mental wellness. Often, if one's mental health is sound, one is more inclined to address health's physical and social aspects as well.

In recent years, the number of people who have become overnight leadership coaches has grown exponentially. However, credibility to lead others through a process of raising their level of self-awareness so that they make critical, credible, creative, and informed leadership decisions and overcome their past hurts or hang-ups requires a thorough understanding of how the mind works. Once that is determined, the way to holistically relate the mind to one's health, wellness, and leadership goals becomes more evident and poignant. I suggest that a coach, especially a leadership health and wellness coach, has to understand the intricacies of cognitive perceptions, interactions, and employment in decision-making and organizational goal setting. Additionally, the coach must work with the leader on the organizational development of those goals if he or she wants to know how they are connected to physical, social, and mental health and wellness.

Cognitive psychology involves the exclusive study of our internal mental processes interacting in our brain. This discipline includes how we perceive our world and what we remember, pay attention to, comprehend in our language, and learn or apply to problem-solving[3]. This measure of knowledge means that one must understand the mind and relate its impact on behavior to organizational-leadership performance in cognitive applications, especially if a leader or entrepreneur is to excel. Mental/spiritual, physical, and social health and wellness are connected to successful leadership in business, health care, education, and ecclesiastic or other organizational

---

[3]   Understanding Brain Science and Cognitive Psychology, accessed April 15, 2022, *https://apa.org/aaction/science/brain-science.*

institutions. Success in any corporate endeavor involves a balance in human systems of consciousness, which addresses sound health and wellness of the organizational leader's cognitive faculties. The decision-making processes and effective execution of any office are based on the efficient interplay of the goals of a healthy and well state of mind and leadership goals.

Corporate and small business leaders, especially among other organizational leaders, are under constant pressure to succeed and keep their heads above water so that their institutions can survive their formative years. Unfortunately, leaders often may not realize that their past hurts and hang-ups, whatever they may be, as well as their unhealthy physical, social, and mental conditions can be carried into their businesses or organizations. This makes them not only inefficient or ineffective—because they're not self-aware—but also consequently unprofitable or unproductive. In a cross-cultural study conducted on Chief Executive Officers' (CEO) leadership performance explored across 24 countries, the astounding results with statistical significance revealed that the tone and behavior of the organization's CEO determined various positive and negative outcomes of the organization.[4] The results suggested that behaviors of these leaders across their respective organizations were consistent with the notion that for those not self-aware of their conduct, there were negative implications in contrast to those who were more self-aware.

This lack of self-awareness among leaders across organizations is the reason that a clearly defined coaching methodology and comprehension of how to work with business, health-care, educational,

---

[4]   House, Robert. J., Peter. W. Dorfman, Mansour. Javidan,, Paul. J. Hanges, & Mary. F. Sully de Luque, (2014). *Strategic leadership across cultures: The GLOBE study of CEO leadership behavior and effectiveness in 24 countries.* Sage Publications, Inc.

or ecclesiastic leaders to transform them and attain leadership success are central to the Connected Cognitive Coaching (Triple C) model for leaders. This model defines coaching as the leadership health and wellness coach's deliberate and mindful effort to elicit thought-provoked responses and behaviors from the coachee-leader, by asking them critical questions based on their mental states of change readiness to successfully achieve professional excellence in decision-making.

To understand why some leaders make consistently flawed decisions, refuse to take certain actions, or are hesitant to act on a specific course of action to raise their level of self-awareness, we must understand that these reservations stem from some potential fears. These fears inhibit performance and create indifference or ambivalence to positive action due to some likely past hurts or personal hang-ups, which reveal themselves in unconscious biases or reservations. When I was going through my introspective moment that day on the bathroom floor, I knew I had to overcome anything that would hold me back from being successful in moving forward in my naval career. I knew I had to decide whether I was going to move on to assume greater responsibilities in the naval service or whether I was going to resolve to settle my passions. I was hung up on the past, yet I had desires for the future. I may have been in good physical and social shape, but I certainly wasn't mentally sound because of the divided loyalties that were present. Such cognitive handicaps form a leadership gap worth exploring with skilled leadership coaching strategies. Nothing like that existed in the professional services of the armed forces, where I honed my leadership prowess. I knew then, just as assuredly as I know now, that if leaders do not take time to align their pasts and presents with their futures, they are bound for a rocky leadership ride.

Leadership and leadership health-and-wellness coaching are used in this context to describe coaching any leader or entrepreneur in a position to run an organization, small business, or enterprise. Understanding how one perceives a notion and processes the thought to apply it actively can be both intricately challenging and sometimes blatantly inexplicable when making sense of one's decision-making to achieve desired goals. Consequently, employing a method that enables deeper access to one's past experiences, which are resident in one's subconscious, and how such experiences or perceptions ultimately impact one's life is essential. Additionally, understanding why some organizational leaders falter in their decision-making processes and their handicap in employing sound leadership strategies to arrive at clearly researched, contemplated, or informed decisions is evident across several organizations and industries. As in sports, a coach's expertise to guide one through and access one's cognitive state so that one can arrive at a heightened level of performance is imperative. A similar paradigm is ideal for leadership development to enable organizational leaders to perform at their peaks.

The connection between the states of mind and the leadership problem of ill-contemplated and ill-informed decision-making is intriguing. Understanding the flawed application of fundamental leadership principles calls for effective techniques or methodologies that bridge the gap between perceiving a notion and performing a decision. Entrepreneurs or service-based leaders, especially among other organizational leaders, must be effective and efficient in assessing how they make these decisions and the net effect of those decisions to affect desired change. The connection between involuntary actions or behaviors and leadership decision-making, with goal setting that affects people at all levels of the leadership continuum, compels a need for leaders to ensure that the decisions they make are not laden with unfiltered notions.

This book posits that leadership development strategies such as leadership coaching methodologies are essential for grooming young and less seasoned leaders, whether in small businesses or otherwise, so that they can channel their efforts and thought processing toward clear and wise decision-making, which is unencumbered by any physical, social, or mental inhibitions. This cognitive coaching model occurs through a three-stage process of uncovering our anxieties, which are insinuated as fears from the unconscious mind, debunking or judging those thoughts by facts in our preconscious mind, and then ultimately manifesting our fantasies in our conscious mind through actions. This method, employed at a lower positional level (management) of leadership or higher, is vital to success, before encountering critical decisions with higher stakes, such as at the chief-executive (C-suite) levels. Therefore, exploring how the mind connects to desired goals (wellness and leadership) is critical. Leadership health and wellness are essential to sound decision-making and goal setting so that one can identify the ideal questions to ask as a leadership health and wellness coach and the way to lead organizational leaders to attain the highest performance level through their cognitive awareness. As the coaching process unfolds, determining the connection between a leader's mental state, health and wellness disposition, and propensity to overcome his or her personal setbacks effectively is a function of how well the leadership health and wellness coach applies the Triple C model to goal setting and attainment. This patient and intentional mind-elicitation approach and the leader's constant quest to remain at peak performance in organizational leadership success are the roles of a well-trained and certified leadership health and wellness coach.

CHAPTER 1

What's the Problem?

Unexpressed emotions will never die. They are
buried alive and will come forth later in uglier ways.

—Sigmund Freud

NOTHING SIGNIFICANT WILL change unless one adequately prepares
to admit there is a problem with the reason that something is the
way it is and that it could be better. No move toward rectifying the
situation will occur if one is not intentional about changing the status
quo. The morning I realized there was a problem in the organization,
which I was to lead as a young and freshly minted naval officer, I
was drenched with a bucket of cold water while sitting on a chair
on the flight deck of my ship. It was a fairly warm afternoon in the
middle of the Atlantic Ocean. I was unprepared and not expecting
what appeared to be an act of humiliation or belittling the new guy
for fun. Some would call that hazing. Others may call it an initiation.

Why would such a ridiculous thing happen to disrupt good order and discipline? After all, I had a team of people I was to be in charge of. How would that go toward earning the due respect I had to work up to? My commanding officer had ordered a young sailor to do so as a form of welcoming the new crew member. If anyone had been malicious or concerned, the incident could have easily turned into a case of hazing, racial discrimination, conduct unbecoming of an officer, or anything else. We had a leader who was defiant of regulations, policies, and in some cases, expected procedures. I didn't know anything then. I was just an ensign in the world's finest naval service. He made his own rules when the established rules worked just fine. He was different, and he was proud of it. Unfortunately, this kind of conduct led to a disturbing and troubled organizational culture, which would scar and mar some likely for life. What was the problem? The leader lacked self-awareness regarding the impacts of his personal conduct toward others because he was neither socially nor mentally healthy enough to lead.

When an organization has a problem, and the people working there are unsettled, displeased, resentful, or flat-out unhappy with how things are, the leader needs to take action and do something. So what's the problem? The problem happens when leaders fall short of being self-aware of their flaws and mandate the performance of their employees or subordinates to feed their whims and caprices. There is a problem when leaders with significant influence, who are in positions of authority, perform with the notion of do as I say, and not as, do I do. Consequently, they make flawed or detrimental decisions. There is a problem when employees, team members, or third parties that are external to the organization perceive, experience, or suggest a systemic cultural issue, which affects organizational performance, and everyone but the organization's leader recognizes it. Often, these problems stem from the leader's cognitive dissonance in his or her personal or professional life. This dissonance may be a result of the absence of the leader's self-care. The research into health-oriented leadership suggests that the extent of a leaders' self-care practices has substantial influence on leadership health effectiveness and team performance, as teams are less stressed and productive, compared to leaders without principles or practices of self-care[5]. This leadership problem of leaders not being self-aware of their own leadership limitations in various aspects including physical, social, and mental or spiritual health may lead to the dissonance that occurs in some organizations.

Cognitive dissonance occurs when one's behaviors or actions contradict what one believes or perceives as a worthy ideal. For instance, a leader knows that a healthy breakfast or a well-rested mind and body are imperative to be effective and alert at work and to make sound decisions. However, the leader takes unhealthy actions, which are not well thought out for sound decision-making. Therefore, a leader cannot be effective without a disciplined health and wellness regimen. The leadership health and wellness term used in this book and in this context is a holistic one, which addresses the healthy decision-making principles of a leader's physical, mental or spiritual, and social well-being, with a focus on mental (cognitive) well-being as the controller of the whole person (conduct and conclusions). When an organization is termed dysfunctional or toxic, it's not because its systems and processes are inefficient and nonfunctional; it is often because the leader or leaders in charge may have created a problematic culture due to an unhealthy life, which bleeds into an unhealthy organization. Pause and reflect for a second on any leader

---

[5]   Klug, Katharina, Jörg Felfe, and Annika Krick. "Does Self-Care Make You a Better Leader? A Multisource Study Linking Leader Self-Care to Health-Oriented Leadership, Employee Self-Care, and Health." *International Journal of Environmental Research and Public Health* 19, no. 11 (May 31, 2022): 6733. https://doi.org/10.3390/ijerph19116733.

you may have known. Then consider the person's background. What do you see? What's the problem?

The problem, then, is not ignorance or dismissal but rather, flawed perceptual notions and an absence of one's self-awareness metric—a measure or method to self-assess one's perceptive effectiveness. This lack of self-awareness impacts sound mental, physical, and social health and wellness—a result of an altered state of mind from what the leader perceives as ideal for leadership success. When this altered state of mind occurs, a leader with cognitive dissonance attempts to justify or mitigate the dissonance with justifications of actions, which blatantly defy logic and facts or often contradict established standards, policies, or regulated outcomes. This is a significant problem, which the cognitive approach to leadership health and wellness coaching attempts to resolve by aiding those caught in this ensnared mental state to overcome the dissonance with consonance (alignment or agreement) so that they can become more effective in their decision-making. Since decision-making is a critical leadership aspect, dissonance almost always emerges if the leader has not developed effective, healthy leadership habits and self-awareness measures to be well and excel.

When leaders are not self-aware or conscious of how their conduct and performance impact their team members, they become loose cannons, which must be restricted, secured, and not positioned to create potential havoc in their path. This is where skilled leadership coaching comes into play and prevents such havoc. Identifying the extent of an issue where a leader appears as the emperor with no clothes requires understanding in how to connect with the leader strategically. As a coach, you must connect on a level that does not undermine their self-esteem and cognitive aptitude so that they can lead uniquely and naturally and without feeling burdened by what others say or think about them. To connect mental states to their conduct, the coach must be prepared, observant, conversant, and passionately interested in his or her leaders' outcome regardless of how obstinate, aloof, or atypical that leader might be. Interest in the leader means determining if a leadership problem hinders performance, productivity, or profitability. Also, finding where the leadership gaps are in the organization, where there may be unconscious biases, or what one may seemingly construe as an attitude of ambivalence to change toward critical and sensitive issues within the organization is essential.

THE LEADERSHIP PROBLEM

Leaders experience several challenges in decision-making, which compel them to seek and synthesize methods and strategies to arrive at well-informed decisions and achieve their desired goals. However, certain preconceived notions, past experiences, personal reservations or biases, insecurities about outcomes, and overall mental health and wellness can preclude sound choices in the decision-making processes. Isn't it strange that research suggests we make approximately two thousand decisions each hour? From when one wakes up in the morning to when one arrives at work, it is quite likely that decisions can work in or against one's favor. Unfortunately, some of these notions can be severe and sometimes costly obstacles to the progression in a professional environment when unchecked by peer accountability and lack of superior decision-making oversight.

A report in one issue of the *Harvard Business Review* indicated that some of the things to look out for when making informed decisions include decision fatigue, over consideration of all the facts that paralyze the decision-making process, and whether the right type or measure of input informs the decision.[6] Therefore, the leadership problem is not the absence of sound decision-making competence but

---

[6]   "Six Reasons We Make Bad Decisions and What to Do about Them," *Harvard Business Review*, August 2019. Retrieved from https://hbr.

the inherent presence of untapped resources, skill sets, and refined methodologies to aid decision-makers in their quest for decisive action because they may not be cognitively healthy. Great leadership and excellence start with a good mind that controls healthy physical and social decisions, which translates into sound decision-making and goal setting. Since we know that the mind controls our actions of physical and social well-being, our health has to start with the mind. A healthy cognitive presence connected to healthy leadership habits, which inform sound decision-making and goal setting, will lead to successful organizations.

Leaders make personal and professional choices every day. The least ones should be decisions about whether they are making the right or sound choice. Yet history records several leaders whose decisions have either cost lives or resulted in ill-conceived fortunes. Decisions by infamous leaders like Kenneth Lay of Enron, Bernard Madoff's Ponzi scheme, and Jeffrey Epstein's alleged sexual misconduct are just a few of such choices. The lack of accountability and recognized leadership oversight strategies, methodologies, and clearly defined outcomes are leadership problems. Techniques and procedures for enhancing decision-making prowess that are not refined result in inadequate or incompetent leadership and leadership performance gaps. These occur especially when and where a moral compass is nonexistent. Some of these decision-making results among the abovementioned cases make headlines every year.

LEADERSHIP GAP

A leadership gap exists in an organization that has systems, processes, or paradigms to enable performance. Yet the respective leader

---

org/2019/08/6-reasons-we-make-bad-decisions-and-what-to-do-about-them.

is either unaware of their interrelatedness or simply misses how to operationalize them for effective organizational performance. In *The Leadership Gap: Building Leadership Capacity for Competitive Advantage*, the authors highlight the lack of action toward building leadership capacity and therefore, leadership strength to leverage the full extent of effectiveness within an organization.[7] The absence of a leadership framework or an effective leadership development process or a flawed approach to leveraging intellectual capital are systemic organizational principles that undermine organizational performance if not effectively addressed.

For instance, an organization struggles to communicate its message to potential clients, customers, or patrons, on how effective it is in employing specific strategies to close the gender leadership gaps in its organizational management. Evidently, this issue becomes a daunting endeavor, which must be explicitly addressed in the organization's models and strategies.[8] Such an organization risks not being viable as its efforts get lost in the sauce of everything else that may not necessarily be relevant to the organization's sustenance. This absence of clarity on purpose and objectivity may indicate a leadership gap that needs addressing within the organization. Therefore, the need for developing a leadership health and wellness coaching protocol or paradigm to overcome such cognitive flaws becomes quite imperative.

---

[7]   David S. Weiss and Vince Molinaro, *The Leadership Gap: Building Leadership Capacity for Competitive Advantage* (John Wiley and Sons, 2010).

[8]   Ellen Kuhlmann, Pavel V. Ovseiko, Christine Kurmeyer, Karin Gutiérrez-Lobos, Sandra Steinböck, Mia von Knorring, Alastair M. Buchan, and Mats Brommels, "Closing the Gender Leadership Gap: A Multi-Centre Cross-Country Comparison of Women in Management and Leadership in Academic Health Centres in the European Union" (*Human Resources for Health*, 2017) 15, no. 1, 1–7.

When identifying leadership gaps within an organization, one need not look far to find the hot spots within the organization. Often, it is hiding in plain sight. One discussion by experts on this topic gleaned from the expert panel of the Forbes Coaches Council was an excerpt titled "10 Ways to Identify Leadership Gaps within Your Company," in which the panel discussed very poignant and salient indicators of a potential problem within the organization.[9] An interpretation of some of the critical highlights they indicated as evidence of leadership gaps are these:

- A stove-piped talented performance with the absence of team collaboration
- A lack of accountability and ownership for missed objectives or requirements
- Seemingly nagging and vocal employees whose concerns may be valid
- Results from 360-degree performance surveys that reveal systemic gaps
- A loss of influence between direct reports and immediate or higher leaders
- When employees are quitting their bosses though they love their jobs

It is not uncommon to identify some, if not all, of these in a dysfunctional organization. Often, primary indicators may be identified during the first contact with an organization's employee or client. Look, bad news, product, or service doesn't go too far before someone hears about it, but it takes time to disseminate good service because it is not only expected but taken for granted.

---

[9] Expert Panel on Forbes Coaches Council, "Ten Ways to Identify Leadership Gaps within Your Company," *Forbes*, May 23, 2019.

THE GAP IN LEADERSHIP AND PERFORMANCE

Part of the problem organizations encounter every day in their boardrooms and engineering plants are the gaps between leadership competence and professional know-how or expertise. Leadership is not a clearly defined or moderately assimilated skill one can pick up without proper comprehension of the context in which it is applied. A leader is only one when someone follows or his or her influence engenders followership of that individual's thoughts, ideas, or direction. In this book's context, leadership refers to anyone who influences another by his or her thoughts, teachings, or conduct to take positive action. Leadership compels a sense of purpose and awakening for either students of the leader's teachings or followers of the leader's vision. Nevertheless, the required action to realize the purpose or vision of leaders remains a significant challenge for many.

Performance refers to a sustained, superior engagement and drive in attaining intended objectives, which lead to evident and proven outcomes. Performance may be mediocre or superior. However, the usual connotation of performance denotes a heightened level of achievement in one's action to warrant superior recognition. When one achieves an objective through driven action, one fulfills a purpose that is only attributed to a desire not to settle for less or to accept a status-quo outcome. This performance is desirable for almost all leaders, but it is challenging to attain without clearly defined goals or objectives. This is why coaching becomes important to remedy the problem or bridge the gap.

There is a gap in effective leadership and performance when the desired achievement level does not meet the superior outcomes expected because the guidance, teachings, influence, or operational conduct to attain them are flawed. When a gap occurs, performance results remain plateaued unless leadership in the specified area of influence or need recognizes a disparity between desired outcomes and the measure of leadership involvement. This plateau can be inconsistent with the desired remarkable achievement. Where such a gap is present, the principles annotated in this book should help bridge leadership with performance and arrive at the expected end—a sustained, superior performance in any professional endeavor. Understanding the essence and power of the subconscious mind and the skill of successfully accessing it through sound personal habits and coaching strategies are essential.

NATURAL FEARS

It is natural for us humans to have inherent fears, which prevent us from being effective at what we do in our self-leadership and in leading others. It is the fear of failure, fear of another's authority over one's own, fear of the unknown, fear of someone finding out how much we actually don't know about a topic, or quite simply, fear of not making the desired impact we would want to make. Often, these fears stem from not having a leadership health and wellness regimen. These fears are natural impulses or conditions we must overcome by a mental state and attitude that attains positive results and not hindered objectives.

Encyclopedias record that we are born with two particular natural fears: the fear of falling and the fear of loud sounds. Interestingly, by the time we outgrow our toddler years, those two fears seem to disappear or dissipate as we learn to walk and understand our environment. This natural state implies that fears can be lost when we learn how to act or think differently about what we fear, using strategies we are taught or adapt to naturally. Today, several adults still have natural or inherent fears such as a fear of flying on airplanes, heights, bugs, or even closed spaces. These phobias can also occur in leadership. The need to have a sound, healthy, and well-rounded leadership approach cannot be overstated.

While in my elementary school years, I had a fear of clowns. For some reason, I associated clowns with monsters, and they were too scary to get close to. At the time, I had no frame of reference or positive encounters and facts about what clowns were to counter my fears or the negative impressions that resided in my subconscious mind. It was not until I turned ten years old that I learned clowns were just people like me, dressed in funny suits or apparel, that I began to ease my reservations and preconceived notions about clowns. How did that fear develop and nurture for so long? It was because of a lack of knowledge. Such fears present potential setbacks to effective leadership. They must be addressed with adequate coaching mechanisms or models as I have attempted to craft them for you across these pages. So you see, what I needed at that tender age were facts about what clowns to counter what I felt or thought they were so that I could effectively relate to them. The same goes for the fear of being ridiculed for a seemingly unhealthy physical appearance due to weight or stature. Soon, we may create our own perception that we are inadequate or ineffective in our leadership.

These natural fears weren't caused by any traumatic experience or specific occurrences that embedded them in our subconscious mind. They may have occurred because we were never taught otherwise, never outgrew them, or were never desensitized from them. As a result, these fears become part of our livelihood, and we accept them as normal or as our fears. (I have a fear of X.) Such fears, if left unchecked, unresolved, or unsuppressed, may potentially become the most inhibiting factors that preclude one from accomplishing one's desired objectives, whether professional or personal. When these fears remain in one's mind, they comfortably and uninhibitedly reside in our subconscious mind until something related to them triggers a response. This state of mind is how we know our real inhibitions and shortcomings regarding fears and the power of the subconscious mind to overrule or overcome them. Fears are instinctive defenses against the discomfort of the unfamiliar, unattractive, undisclosed, or undesired. Until one has learned and allowed time and exposure to the fear, one remains in a conundrum of fearful states, which preclude action and sound decision-making. Consequently, if left unchecked and unaddressed, these perceptive notions unwittingly grow into unconscious biases. They become biases in our leadership approach.

UNCONSCIOUS BIASES AND EFFECTS

As we grow into our respective social cultures, nurturing environments, and belief systems, we carry our perceptions of how things are or should be. We form opinions, arguments, defenses, and beliefs about what we deem to be true and worthy of exploration. As a young adult, I learned several things from the environment I was nurtured in. I held onto beliefs that shaped my mindset of what I thought about people who did not look like, believe like, or act like me, such as those who were born with a gender disposition opposite of what they currently portray. When some of these beliefs we hold to be true are infringed on or are questioned, the triggers to defend or uphold our prevalent state of mind become necessary. Science calls such purported notions and impressions, which are deeply embedded in the subconscious mind, unconscious biases. They are unconscious because they reside in our minds without intention. We take action on such intentions based on our perception or thought process, which social scientists call biases.

In some cases, these biases can be detrimental and self-limiting if not properly researched, understood, or informed. Biases are not only challenging to dismiss or destroy but can also be systemic and self-serving. Preferences in prejudice enable those who hold them to resent anything contrary to what the belief system naturally suggests. If left unchecked, such mental states may become evident in speech, conduct, performance, and in some cases, the judgment of others. For instance, among the several types of biases are an affinity bias, which refers to the tendency of a person to gravitate toward people similar to himself or herself, whether in creed, color, credibility, or craze. Another is a conformity bias, which occurs typically in group settings when one's action is compelled or influenced by the actions or tendencies of the majority, who conform to a specific trend. Worse yet among leaders is the halo effect, which is a bias that tends to place one on a pedestal of impressive achievement, which implies perceived excellence in all aspects of attainment without validating competence and performance in those unrelated areas. If misrepresented or miscommunicated in an organization by any leader responsible or accountable for others' well-being, these biases may present significant setbacks, drawbacks, and paybacks, which may be unwelcome. Consequently, to alleviate this leadership problem, understanding how to mitigate and potentially eliminate such conditions effectively is imperative for every leader. Any desired action that confuses the leader may be due to conflicting positions from his or her fears, which causes ambivalence.

AMBIVALENCE TO CHANGE

Some leaders tend to ignore a problem by pretending it doesn't exist or assuming that it is someone else's problem to solve later. The "That's the way we've always done it," or "If it's not broken, don't fix it" syndrome is both disheartening and unacceptable for any leader, let alone an effective and competent leader. One need not look too far to discover a host of social ambivalence to change, which permeates leadership positions across organizations. Accepting the status quo as the norm and giving attention to what is baseless and less significant over what is critical, such as amicable and purposeful human relations instead of who the next client, patient, or prospect is and what that person has to offer the organization, are fair examples.

When a leader is ambivalent to any changes or modifications in decision-making or active responses to issues or conditions, it is likely an indication of burnout or cop-out to make up for what he or she cannot do for whatever reason or circumstances that hold that individual back. Understanding how to assist or help such leaders effectively is everyone's responsibility. Such leaders may very well be on the verge of a depressive and in some cases, dangerous mental state, which may place their team, followers, or organization in peril. Ambivalence, therefore, is a significant problem for a leader. It may spell the need for an external source of cognitive stimulation—in this case, you, the coach—to get the leader out of the valley that he or she may be stuck in.

It is not that a leader is incapable of leading or is incompetent in his or her role, but rather, at some point in a leader's life, he or she may present a state of mind where that person becomes too caught up in themselves, overwhelmed by the environment, unmoved by the circumstances, or unaware of the gravity of his or her role. This condition may occur for various reasons, which require someone else like an expert, specialist, or a leadership health and wellness coach to assist the leader in recognizing and acknowledging that individual's present state. The assistance will enable the leader to become more effective and aware of the demands of his or her leadership role. Consequently, addressing such a problem requires effective and enduring coaching strategies and methodologies, which bring value to the leader. Therefore, understanding where a leader may be stuck and needs help to get unstuck requires understanding and interpreting the leadership mind.

CHAPTER 2

How to Interpret the Leadership Mind

What we see changes what we know.
What we know changes what we see.

—Jean Piaget (Swiss psychologist)

WHEN ONE THINKS of the leadership mind, what comes to mind? No pun is intended. Is it a center of cognitive awareness? Is it a personal space where one can manufacture who one really is? Does the mind reveal what one can achieve, what one can direct, and what one could ultimately become? I would argue *yes* to all the above. The mind is a powerhouse. Some estimate that the brain, the seat of our mind or thought, can process thought as fast as a sprinter responds to a starting gun, which is about 150 milliseconds (perceived as 35–120 meters per second).[10] Though this speed is several times slower than a computer's is, it is also relatively fast for a human to think and process information. However, this cognitive processing can occur efficiently only when one is uninhibited by other factors that preclude one from thinking clearly and performing at one's highest peak. I am certain no one will argue this premise. Without a sound mind, one is frankly nonexistent. By nonexistent, I mean unable to function socially, professionally, or often personally. This dysfunction is the reason that when one does something perceived as socially or professionally unacceptable, one is likely to hear the expression, "You must be out of your mind!" As harsh and concerning as this might be, the mind is one of the most precious and powerful personal assets that one must employ to the greatest extent possible. Employment of the mind involves being healthy and well so that one can develop one's level of self-awareness. To do so means efficiently using one's state of mind, learning how to shift paradigms, and understanding that paradigms take a developing and strong mind to conceive. Being able to lead others into very challenging yet rewarding feats takes a particularly demanding and powerful mindset to attain. Therefore, understanding how the mind works, how it should work, or what prevents it from working effectively is critical for every leader.

THE CURIOUS MIND

When I was in grade school and beyond, I had a curious mind, which always desired to know why I couldn't achieve any desire, goal, or challenge that any teacher, instructor, or professor presented. I once asked a teacher why some people were called smart, and others were

---

[10] Christian Jarrett, "What Is the Speed of Thought?" *Science Focus*, retrieved from *http://www.sciencefocus.com/the-human-body/what-is-the-speed-of-thought/*.

inappropriately called slow. I asked why all people could not be considered smart based on their measure of application. Why couldn't students be graded intellectually by their level of effort in the areas they showed and felt they were most skilled and exceptionally effective or gifted? That quest for clarity on perception and mindset gave the class a new perspective on brilliance—the notion that everyone is brilliant at something. Something one is uniquely and naturally gifted in, therefore, must be introspectively sought to redefine smartness and slowness. I would argue that this effort to be vocal and lead the class to a new way of thinking could arguably reflect a leadership mind—a mind willing to question the unquestioned and challenge the status quo in word or deed.

One of the greatest authors and mindset motivational speakers of all time, Napoleon Hill, of *Think and Grow Rich* (TAGR) fame, said it quite succinctly: "Whatever the mind can conceive and believe, it can achieve." I would add that if one is ready and willing to receive their God-given purpose or gifts, that statement can be modified as whatever one is willing and ready to conceive and receive, one must believe to achieve it. This is strictly an inherent communication amongst one's mind, heart, and soul. The reception of thought in this context denotes an unencumbered acceptance of one's life's purpose, which mainly and unequivocally occurs only when one has come to terms with who one is as a person and as an exceptional contributor to the human race. Many often sell themselves short, undermine their capabilities and capacities to excel, and accept mediocrity and limiting mindsets as their portion or lot in life. Today, Napoleon Hill's book *Think and Grow Rich* has made more millionaires than any other book historically attributed or recorded. So when such a condition persists, you have not received your life's purpose, and therefore, you will be hindered by what you can conceive in your mind, let alone believe. Therefore, your mind is the factory of your brilliance, and your brilliance is the foundation of your life's excellence. Search for, protect, nourish, and use it.

As a theoretical physicist, many considered Albert Einstein one of the most powerful minds that ever lived. His theory of general relativity, as we learned in high school, and its impact on furthering science research can only be admired and appreciated by scientists today because it paved the way for notions like quantum physics and other scientific research. Why is this reference essential? Suppose energy and its relationship with mass and light, which is calculated as $E=mc^2$, is acceptable for everyone to understand as something of relevance derived from a scientist's mind? It goes to show that anyone can think and develop something of value for others to use as long as it is impactful. This is where leadership's power and authority reside and the reason the mind is such an invaluable resource. It should never be taken for granted by anyone, no matter who one is or where one falls in the continuum of leadership or personal development. To employ the mind to be effective and perform at its best, a leader needs room or time in space to think. Although thinking is fundamental and effortless, it begs the application of one's inherent strengths, desires, ambitions, and expectations to make the thought, whatever that might be, worthwhile. Consequently, one's environment is the fundamental and most important place to assess the viability of thought.

THE COGNITIVE ENVIRONMENT

When considering an environment for growing crops, herbs, or flowers, one considers an environment free of problems or obstacles to achieve the desired goals of bearing fruit or a harvest. Similarly, when a team or organization's leader considers an environment for achieving his or her goals, that individual determines how and when to attain the desired goal. This may occur as a personal desire as the leader contemplates in the convenience of a home or office, or the leader might solicit a think tank or mastermind alliance to help think through the desired outcome. Whatever approach is employed, the leader needs an environment that allows thought to occur and clear, unbiased, unadulterated, and unencumbered thought to thrive. This is what I call the cognitive environment.

A highly toxic cognitive or intellectually lopsided environment means more technocrats than bureaucrats or philosophers will yield a seemingly one-sided outcome. An environment where leaders can think freely about how best to lead and tap into their intellectual repertoires demands critical self-awareness. An environment that does not provide serenity and clarity of purpose and intent will hurt and distort the mind's efforts to think. A healthy cognitive environment nourishes clear goals and objectives, no external stimuli or pressure from any professional or social source, and no personal nuances or agendas that could potentially derail or adversely affect the outcome of the leader's thought objectives.

Katherine Johnson, who is an American mathematician and considered one of the most powerful and brilliant minds of the space race, excelled in helping transform one of NASA's greatest historical operations: launching astronaut John Glen into space.[11] Because her nurture environment was limited by racial segregation of the time, her intellectual prowess was not validated until she could exercise her cognitive aptitude. The rationale here is that she recognized her giftedness and knack for numbers. She sought mentorship from another brilliant man, math professor W. W. Schieffelin Claytor, who was the third African American ever awarded a PhD. Though the segregation environment appeared challenging, and it did not foster opportunities for enhancing performance for African Americans at the time, Johnson's desire to excel and passion for numbers drove her

---

[11]   "Katherine Johnson's Biography," retrieved from *https://www.nasa.gov/content/katherine-johnson-biography.*

into action and pro-action. She consequently made the most of her intellect. She would later become a force multiplier and instrumental asset to the nation's space program. What does this say about the cognitive environment? One can almost always have the mind of excellence and competence. Still, one needs an opportunity to express it. This is why the right climate for cognitive expression is essential.

In a McKinsey study of several chief executive officers, effectiveness and best practices from their mindsets revealed that they set up the office of a special or executive assistant and a chief of staff. They enabled sorting out of priorities and allowance of alone time to think and prepare for daily objectives.[12] This study revealed that what made CEOs excellent was not being superhuman or super busy, but it included, among several other strategies, the need to make time and a place to think. This place and time to think creates an environment conducive to thought leadership and excellence. Such an environment must not only yield an opportunity to thrive and excel but also a forum open for feedback and constructive performance critique. An environment that fosters a mechanism for such introspection and reflection is certain to remedy errors or mismanagement before it festers into misfortune.

So what does this mean for leaders who may have several competing requirements and multiple issues to think through because they have not developed a mechanism or system that enables thought leadership? If that is you, four approaches will jump-start seeking a cognitive environment to free your mind and time for reflection. They are based on the acrostic SELF: seek, empower, learn, and foster.

---

[12] Carolyn Dewar, Hirt Martin, and Keller Scott, "The Mindsets and Practices of Excellent CEOs," October 25, 2019, retrieved from *https://www.mckinsey.com/business-functions/strategy-and-corporate-finance/our-insights/the-mindsets-and-practices-of-excellent-ceos#.*

1. **Seek:** Look for a specific time and place to consistently and faithfully be uninterrupted to do your thinking.

2. **Empower:** Find one or two team members. (If you are alone, you are not leading anyone but yourself.) You can delegate some of your most critical tasks and efforts.

3. **Learn:** Discover and understand what new ways and strategies you can employ to enhance your cognitive aptitude and intellectually self-improve.

4. **Foster:** Create a workplace for professional growth and collaboration, where decisions can occur at the lowest leadership level without your direct input. A measure of your effectiveness is the measure of decisive action in your absence.

To create a cognitive environment, you must create a team interdependence culture. Remember, leaders lead best when others lead to their best!

POWER OF INTELLECTUAL STIMULATION

Intellectual stimulation is when a leader encourages followers to stretch their imagination toward innovative and problem-solving initiatives. This leadership approach not only stimulates the mind to do more than it thinks it can do but also allows the leader to leverage followers' expertise, intellect, and performance. Often, leaders find themselves more interested in tapping into the expertise of followers than contributing to ensuring that the health and wellness of followers are adequately nurtured or enhanced to perform at their peak. When a leader makes every effort to stimulate and encourage discovery, that leader significantly increases his or her leadership potential and scope of excellence.

In a study conducted on the influence of intellectual-stimulation leadership behavior on employee performance among small- and medium-sized enterprises in the African country of Kenya, the research revealed a strong, positive, and statistically significant correlation between the leaders' intellectually stimulating behavior and employee performance.[13] The integrity of the research methodology and results demonstrated the reliability of the research to imply that regardless of the type of industry, leaders' intellectual stimulation was imperative to affect the desired innovative and transformational results needed to excel. However, it is essential to note that a leader cannot reach that measure or level of intellectually stimulating behavior if the leader lacks the impetus, drive, or standard of self-awareness to elicit such inspiration within the organization. The onus on the organizational leader to lead and drive transformation compels a high state of cognitive health to reach peak performance. Consequently, if as a leader, you find yourself constrained or confused about whether or not you are practical and impactful in your performance, you must seek opportunities to clear your mind to be highly valuable for your organization.

The power of intellectual stimulation is in the knowledge that when a leader has a sound mind and peak performance because the mind is refreshed, revived, and redirected, the opportunities for growth and clarity of purpose yield innovative and challenged team members. They are well-poised to take action on desired organizational outcomes. Ensuring that as a leader, you are well-rested, unencumbered in thought and action, and assisted in the execution of operational deliverables is very important and undoubtedly imperative for organizational success.

------

[13]   Mary G. O. Ogola, D. Sikalieh, and T. K. Linge, "The Influence of Intellectual Stimulation Leadership Behavior on Employee Performance in SMEs in Kenya," *International Journal of Business and Social Science*, March 2017, 8 (3).

CHAPTER 3

What's the Connection between the Problem and the Leadership Mind?

The major difference between rats and people is that rats learn from experience.

—B. F. Skinner (American psychologist)

THE RELATIONSHIP BETWEEN the problem at hand and the power of the leadership mind lies in two fundamental precepts: What one considers a problem because it is outside one's locus of control, and one's intellectual or intuitive capacity to address thoughts and impulses. The balance between these two actions or inactions within the locus of control and within one's cognitive landscape or room for thought determines how cognitively healthy one is. If you react vehemently or aggressively to sudden changes within your sphere of influence, your responses to problems are dramatic and significant. If you take time to assess, review, and adapt to a strategy that implements actions to sudden changes in your life, your approach to life's challenges is gradual and systematic. In either case, they are cognitively influenced. This relationship between your mind as a leader and any problem you face forms the basis or seat of your cognitive health. It is important to remember that your problem is subordinate to your intellect and never the other way around. As long as it is within your locus of control, you can overcome the problem. Some define this state of mind as your sanity. The *Merriam-Webster Dictionary* defines sanity as "the quality or state of being sane." Sane is defined as "proceeding from a sound mind" or "mentally sound." Additionally, it is always essential to remember that you control how you feel, respond, or direct any external actions around your sphere of influence. No one or nothing can control the impact on your emotions or thoughts without you relinquishing control of the stimulus to that external entity or situation.

As a leader, there will be several moments of doubt, opportunities for indecision, and periods of a lack of clarity in circumstances, which will enable sound decision-making. However, having a strong foundation of key leadership principles that guide your conduct and exercising a daily approach to the way you handle any situation will ensure optimal mental health when an adverse problem arises that you have to act upon. It is like the training that soldiers or marines have to do consistently and sometimes almost daily to condition their minds and bodies in preparation for a battle whenever that should occur. One does not wake up one day and roll right into battle without mental conditioning or rehearsal. Such an approach is one sure way for professional suicide. Similarly, a leader cannot effectively excel and be at peak performance without a consistently conditioned and positively nurtured mental attitude, which cultivates ways and means to adapt and overcome unprecedented, unclear, and unfamiliar circumstances. It takes unique resourcefulness to become mildly proficient should an adverse situation challenge your cognitive resilience and aptitude to excel and bring transformational change or impact to the problem. For instance, as a leader, if you have not trained yourself and those you influence for a tragedy such as an active-shooter scenario within your organization, your responses to the situation before, during, and after it occurs may be devastating. It will be traumatic for you and others because of the sheer mental toll it will take on you. Practice, proficiency, and providence are the saving graces of unprecedented and unlikely natural disasters or social traumas. To condition and prepare your mind for unlikely and unexpected times, the two approaches that may be essential to raise your measure of resilience and cognitive aptitude to lead are

1. How you perceive and respond to the problem
2. How you employ the strategies and methods that you have at your disposal to affect the desired outcomes

I refer to these two approaches as the positive mental attitude of Napoleon Hill fame and resourcefulness, which is another essential leadership attribute.

POSITIVE MENTAL ATTITUDE (PMA)

Napoléon Hill calls this optimistic state of mind positive mental attitude (PMA). It is an invaluable approach to resolve especially trying and cognitively obtuse circumstances, but it also provokes opportunities to explore avenues that would otherwise be left unexamined. PMA provides hope for the seemingly hopeless and creates pathways where obstacles once thrived. Henry Ford once said, "Whether you think you can, or you think you can't, you're right." This quote speaks to the heart of having a PMA. Two notable figures that come to mind are Steve Jobs, who was initially removed from his own company at Apple due to too many failed projects, and Oprah Winfrey, who overcame an abusive and traumatic childhood and adolescence to become one of the world's wealthiest and notable television figures.[14] The lesson here is that no matter the challenge, what you do with the circumstance you face determines how well you can place in the race. Never allow your past conditions or dictations to shape your present circumstances or your future endeavors. It only worsens an already troubled and fragile state of mind.

PMA, then, provides the individual an opportunity to look at a given problem through a lens that offers options to make what would otherwise be a hopeless and bleak situation seem a worthy challenge and endeavor.

RESOURCEFULNESS

I will argue that resourcefulness is the ability to make things happen during challenging and bleak times, using any sources, methods, strategies, or measures you can to attain the desired results. Now you would agree with me, wouldn't you, that every leader should be capable of honing this skill and using it effectively to his or her advantage if the leader wants to be exceptionally impactful in any sphere of influence? What sometimes appears impossible for leaders is the application of resourceful strategies to arrive at their desired outcomes. Sometimes, those outcomes are not readily apparent or clearly defined. For instance, to be resourceful, a leader must be proficient at knowing where to seek help in terms of systems, pro-

---

[14] Jayson Demers, "Seven Challenges Courageous Leaders Overcome," *Inc.*, September 9, 2014, retrieved from *https://www.inc.com/jayson-demers/7challenges-courageous-leaders-overcome.html.*

cesses, partner organizations, programs, regulations, or fundamental procedures to help the team succeed.

As a leader, you must be proficient in the methodologies or strategies to influence and communicate effectively with those you lead. This implies you must be people-oriented enough to employ skills like one-on-one meetings, attentive and active listening, active empathy, and providing active support where needed to earn the trust and confidence of those you lead. The first part of this resourcefulness paradigm may come easier to some, but the latter part is not quite as easy because it takes the active engagement of the other party to find out intricate details of what that person needs if you want to be able to help him or her adequately.

In combat or in the heat of an active shooter's sudden attack on an otherwise quiet neighborhood, everything you know about routine or rationale disappears. You quickly have to adapt to an ever-changing and fluid situation in response to the environment that it is occurring in. This is where the mettle of leadership is tried. If I am breaching a door for a target that I am supposed to secure, and I have a team of armed, military-trained men and women with me, my trust and confidence are in their abilities to execute orders and guidance based on my leadership expertise. If the briefed plan of execution to breach that door changes upon arrival to the target door because we realize what was supposed to be a door is now a concrete cemented wall, the whole plan shifts in an instance. No amount of previous planning and strategic mapping will resolve the sudden change in circumstances. Your resourcefulness must kick in regarding how you will effectively and successfully breach that wall to secure the intended target. What will you do, leader, if you ever find yourself in that situation? Ah! You see what I mean. You must know instinctively if there are other ways, means, or methods to accomplish the same objective. In this case, you must secure the target if the door is unbreachable because it is now a wall. The decision to employ another strategy occurs in a matter of seconds because life and limb are at stake. This is why repetition, rehearsal, and cognitive fortitude are significant for a leader to possess so that he or she can be most successful in a most trying time.

THE CORE OF THE RELATIONSHIP

Whether personal or professional, every relationship has to be mutually nurtured and diligently protected to ensure healthy outcomes and productivity for both parties. The essence of a sound relationship between resolving encountered problems and a healthy mind is that the mind must be well-prepared, trained, and conditioned to address any measure of the challenge it meets without being overwhelmed and distressed by its magnitude or gravity. This kind of cognitive resilience does not occur overnight or in a vacuum. It often requires a systematic approach to employing mental drills and methodical reasoning and exposing one's own life to periods of psychological or emotional risk to build the required fortitude to overcome the challenge.

In the United States of America, the military's special warfare contingent of the navy is called SEALs, an acronym that stands for sea, air, and land (SEAL). Candidates for the Special Forces undergo rigorous training to build a relationship between their mental or cognitive acuity and the kind of challenges encountered. Some of these may include being dropped into frigid waters for a swim. Others may be ocean swims followed by runs that strain your body. During these periods, yelling and screaming that mimic enemy captive situations are the norm. The distinction between success and failure during this resilience process boils down to one phrase: the will to survive. The training pipeline is about a seventy-two-week process. It involves mental and physical conditioning, including exposure to physically challenging and stressful environmental elements, which stress your mental faculties and fortitude. Richard Marcinko, a former Navy

SEAL, said, "If your training is properly intense, it will kill you. More often—much, much, more often—it will save your life."[15]

The Navy SEAL handbook clearly articulates the notion that the inclination and propensity for survival solely rest with one's attitude. Why is it important to understand that the mind is your most powerful tool or resource in your arsenal for professional excellence? It is important because without overcoming any mental blocks or preconceived mindsets about your capability or capacity to be successful as a leader in your organization, you will almost assuredly never make it past waking up in the morning to conquer your world. You must believe, know, and act like you do to excel and achieve success in whatever endeavor you undertake. This means attaining one's desire, hope, efforts, and vision of making it to one's desired goal—to stay alive and well through the SEAL training of your mind and the problems you encounter. This is the kind of mindset that every leader needs to overcome to face circumstances that may pose a potential threat or a strain on the mind. Unfortunately, it compels one to think less of one's capacity to endure conditions that seem dire and cognitively untenable due to what one perceives.

The core of the leadership mind-problem relationship rests on the seat of your mindset conditioning and preparation for cognitive combat. Until you cultivate a culture of resilience and sustenance of your mind, body, and spirit (drive), you will have difficulty addressing the desired or expected outcomes in great detail. For instance, if you have to decide between whether to stop and help an injured and immobile person during a random active-shooter situation or to run away from the threat source to alert others to escape, that kind of grave decision and ambivalence in decisive action could weigh

---

[15]   Don Mann and Ralph Pezzullo, *The U.S. Navy SEAL Survival Handbook: Learn the Survival Techniques and Strategies of America's Elite Warriors* (Skyhorse Publishing, 2012).

on your mind for a long time. These thoughts can linger well after the incident is over, especially if the outcome is fatal and traumatic for those you lead. The power of mindset conditioning and your approach to compartmentalizing post-traumatic effects and daily life operations are keys to dealing with such dire instances.

APPLICATION OF THE LEADERSHIP MIND-PROBLEM RELATIONSHIP

In determining how to cope or deal with how you can condition your mind to address the diverse circumstances that you may encounter as a leader in your sphere of influence, taking notes from the Navy SEAL handbook to apply to your professional or personal life is not only prudent but also pragmatic. Few, if any, are trained as well as SEALs to make sound and life-changing decisions as part of their livelihood. Therefore, my application of the leadership mind-problem relationship stems from the modification of the SEALs' SURVIVAL acrostic, which stands for

S: Size up the situation (surroundings, physical condition, and equipment).
U: Use all your senses.
R: Remember where you are.
V: Vanquish fear and panic.
I: Improvise.
V: Value living.
A: Act like the natives.
L: Live by your wits, but for now, learn basic skills.[16]

---

[16]   Ibid.

Adopting the rationale and mindset of this acrostic, I urge you to consider the same perspective for your professional life as a leader. When faced with a stressful and dire decision or dilemma, apply the following leader survival approach:

S: Stop and assess actions for mental clarity.

U: Understand the situation and available options.

R: Remember that lives are first, and mission is always.

V: Verify the legitimacy of available options, sources, and desired outcomes.

I: Identify a course of action and lead it purposefully and intentionally to attain results.

V: Visit and get involved in the efforts for the desired outcomes.

A: Allow recommendations, perspectives, and directions from others.

L: Learn from your mistakes, missteps, and misgivings to inform the future for success.

This acrostic provides you, as the executive leader, a systematic approach and preplanned response to any immediate challenge you face without being frantic and thrown into mental disorientation. Your objective in this mind-and-problem situation is always to give the problem the attention it deserves and adequately assess how much time and resources you require to provide the measure of impact and results you desire. Having this routine and preconditioned approach enables quicker and more purposeful outcomes, which are informed by your tested and proven process.

SCENARIO: THE ACTIVE-SHOOTER
LEADERSHIP DILEMMA

You are the chief executive officer of a consulting and publishing firm with twenty-five full-time employees. You are sitting in your office, which is 250 feet from the main entrance of your building. Suddenly, you hear gunshots coming from what seems to be the direction of the main entrance. You know you have a receptionist and no security in your building. Your immediate actions are

S: Stop work for a second to assess what you are hearing and the immediate actions to take. You *must* have the will to survive this attack. Think and calm your mind.

U: Understand what options you have to escape and survive the gunfire: Exits, active shooter drill, barricade locations, calling 911 or whatever your emergency service number is, self-defense, and anything else that comes to mind to survive.

R: Remember, lives first, so you have to think about your team by determining where everyone is. The training you have put in place before the incident should inform everyone, yet as you exit your office, you see a person lying on the floor in the distance. Those who are seemingly alive, running, and hiding have priority. Search them out and clear rooms immediately.

V: Verify if anyone has called the emergency number by calling it yourself. Never assume someone else has. Go through as many rooms or cubicles as you can on your way out of the back door or hiding place.

I: Identify what actions you will take if you have to fight the attacker before authorities arrive. Designate who, when, and where you will take the action.

V: Visit (get involved) in the actions that will attack or disengage the attacker.

A: Allow others or authorities to do their jobs before you get involved if you know they are more proficient, trained, and informed than you are.

L: Learn from policy decisions, the preplanned responses of your team, and what you could have done better to prepare for such an incident in the future. Don't overlook this step. Stay engaged and informed.

Understanding the relationship between the mind and any problem encountered takes comprehension of self and the situation. Self means being self-aware of your limitations, capabilities, and measure of influence. Situation means understanding thoroughly what the situation entails or presents to make the most informed decision. The key to adequately framing and addressing a resolution to the problem requires sound cognitive health and performance. This can almost always be enhanced and exercised with active coaching and training strategies. Always remember to improve yourself so that you can improve others. It starts with your mind.

CHAPTER 4

Is Your Subconscious Mind the Connector?

> Until you make the unconscious conscious,
> it will direct your life and you will call it fate.
>
> —Carl Jung (Swiss psychiatrist)

IS YOUR SUBCONSCIOUS mind the connector between a healthy mind and leadership success? To adequately answer that question, bringing the subconscious mind to full awareness means accessing the unconscious through the preconscious to the conscious, so that one can fully disclose one's state of awareness regarding how leadership success depends on the sound health and wellness of the leader. This awareness comprises both intrinsic and extrinsic impulses (stimuli), which suggests specific modes of behavior or thought to enable one's actions. To enhance clarity on what the subconscious is, a simplistic definition from the *Merriam-Webster Dictionary* states that it is "existing in the mind but not immediately available to consciousness" or "the mental activities just below the threshold of consciousness." Based on both definitions, it is evident that the subconscious mind is nothing more than the presence of a notion, mindset, belief, thought, image, and name one desires to give to something that lurks in one's psyche (mind). A careful study of the mind-behavior relationship reveals subtle clues to the reason that if one can tame and control the mind, one can conquer humankind. By that, I mean one can know and understand how to live with others and attain one's desired goals. The mind is subject to the heart. What one desires wholeheartedly, one can attain, as long as the two are uniquely synched together with resources that can enable action. Addressing what I call the connector is critical to understanding the power of the subconscious mind. This means understanding how to overcome one's self-limiting belief systems and triggers to transformational change or dysfunctional status quo by being intuitive and perceptive to others and any external stimuli.

THE CONNECTOR

When I talk of the connector, I refer to the intuitive response and engagement with your intrinsic and extrinsic impulses, which are held captive by your subconscious mind and compel you to either take action or inaction on a convincing notion. It involves active listening—connecting. For instance, my intuition compels me to naturally listen to what someone is not saying by attentively picking up on the details they reveal in dialogue, either repeatedly or by constantly avoiding the topic. The *Collins Dictionary*, among others, defines *intuition* as "the power of perception beyond the five senses; sixth sense." Intuition here means being attentive to having a trained ear and mind so that you can connect and effectively pick up such unheard or unclear notions that are indirectly communicated. That skill as a leadership health and wellness coach requires practice, self-awareness, and sensitivity to how one's environment may affect what one hears or comprehends.

If as a leader, your mind is cluttered with all kinds of unsettled thoughts, your body is tired, and your relationships are strained, the chances are that you will not be effective and at your performance peak. You are not healthy and well enough to lead. For instance, I employed my intuitive approach to hear what a young man I was mentoring was saying in a conversation I had with him. He was an international student in the United States with his family and was on the verge of completing his studies. This man was very eager and anxious for my mentorship and guidance. As I had my initial conversation with him to begin the mentorship relationship, it became readily apparent that he was looking for an opportunity to find where he fit into the American economy and what kind of work he could do after graduating from college with an MBA degree. However, in one sitting, the desire for professional mentorship quickly evolved into a desire to do what I do, shadow me as I work, attend my events, participate in my events, and spend as much time as possible with me to get to know him.

Though there was no harm in the desire and intent, the real crux of this man's need was a desire for a career. However, he neither clearly articulated that need nor knew what he wanted to do. By the end of the hour and a half initial mentorship meeting, having a keen intuitive disposition based on my own sense of awareness of my subconscious mind and demonstrating an aptitude for cognitive coaching interplayed well in this situation, it was apparent that the young man needed to find a career to pursue. He didn't know how, so he sought out the mentorship program the university had to launch his quest for self-discovery. You see, I picked up on that from the get-go because I had sharpened and shaped my intuitive impulses to be attentive to what hurts and triggers actions or inactions. As a leadership coach, exercising my intuition (the connector) to pick apart, decipher, and detect any underlying sentiments or resentments that one may harbor helps you determine the course of action or methodology to bring someone through a challenging or seemingly impossible professional task.

Extrasensory perception (ESP) is a phenomenon defined by parapsychologists as a manner of human or animal receipt of information without normal or sensory means.[17] They argue that almost everyone at one time or another experienced this phenomenon based on parapsychological laboratory research conducted so far. Call it what you will—hunch, energy, vibe, or gut feeling, but it boils down to extrasensory perception. Have you ever considered how you communicate with your dog or pet? How do dogs hear and respond to what you tell them? Is it only by positive-behavior reinforcement or sensory communication between a human and a nonhuman? I would argue that this ESP forms the basis of how humans communicate without vocalizing intent. As parapsychologists such as Sigmund Freud described it, this intriguing notion is evident, especially during childhood. It gradually dissipates as humans rely more and more on traditional modes of communication. They suggest that methods such as telepathy were methods by which individuals understood one another and communicated intents and actions. It is not surprising then to understand the communication that occurs, for instance, when a parent looks at a child sternly or when one looks another in the eyes precisely as if to communicate a message. For instance, what does love at first sight really mean between the two would-be lovers? Thinking of someone just before the person calls, receiving

---

[17]   "Extrasensory Perception: The 'Sixth Sense,'" retrieved from *https:// www.encyclopedia.com/science/ncyclopedias-almanacs-transcripts-and-maps/ extrasensory-perception-sixth-sense.*

the response to a question even before you have asked it, as well as buying someone a gift only to discover that person has been seriously considering buying that item are clear indicators of the phenomenon. Researchers refer to versions of these notions as telepathy, psycho-kinesis, precognition, clairvoyance, or the like.

It is important to distinguish the context of the phenomena mentioned above from the context of this writing. In the context of ESP pertaining to leadership health and wellness coaching, the coach employs intuition, a strong perception, or a sense of connection with the person one is communicating with. No premonition, telepathy, or parapsychological innuendos mentioned are at play, except the way the coach employs an understanding of one's mind or mental state to comprehend where one might mentally be fully present at a given time. Nevertheless, it bears mentioning that two parties can communicate effectively without uttering a word, just as one can sense impulses without active or vocal communication of thoughts and intents. Some refer to this in the urban language as energy, whether positive or negative. I have always wondered how other forms of creation communicate without uttering sounds or how humans learn to initiate hugs without informing each other. The point is that how we communicate can affect the measure of responsiveness or non-responsiveness we obtain from one another. I have often referred to my own experiences on this notion of ESP in other parts of this book or other literature.

Before the age of the internet, cell phones, and payphones for long-distance calls, there was snail mail—long handwritten letters in an envelope that you placed stamps on to send across oceans to your recipient. Do you remember those? Some have no idea what I am talking about. Others do. If fortunate, it would be weeks before they would receive your letter. Well, that was how I courted my wife—over a long-distance relationship as I served in the United States Navy. I wrote letters with questions requesting answers to our relationship.

Sometimes, before I could even go to the post office to mail the letter, she would have answered the question or discussed the topic I was referring to in a letter. Now, how does this occur? Call it what you will.

THE SUBCONSCIOUS MIND

We are already aware that the subconscious mind is the thought, image, or word that lurks around our inner being. It is only tapped or accessed when triggered by an act that must be brought to our conscious awareness or present state. Following an article published in *The New York Times* about a study by Yale University psychologists revealing that humans are primed to respond to social cues or behaviors already inherent or prominent to achieve goals or objectives, several studies confirmed the phenomenon.[18] The researchers suggested that people's unconscious choices and the reasoning for their behaviors account for why one can be pleasant in one instance and quickly become obnoxious in another instance. They argued that this shift in behavior results from the interactions between our conscious awareness and unconscious behavioral guidance systems. It is interesting to note how the unconscious mind behaves when notions are suggested to it. For instance, in the same issue of the report, eighteen men and women playing a computer game for money were told to squeeze tighter on the handgrip they were holding whenever an image of money flashed across the screen to keep more of the money. Not surprisingly, they squeezed the handgrip harder each time they saw an image of money flash by, no matter how quickly or superficially that image might have been displayed. This mind–hand coordination reveals the spontaneous

---

[18] Benedict Carey, "Who's Minding the Mind?" *The New York Times*, July 21, 2007.

reaction that occurs even unconsciously once one has in mind what action or inaction one would take on an intended thought.

Consequently, the subconscious mind responds to triggers that allow you to see what is otherwise unseen or buried deep in the mind until compelled to come out without your active awareness. The subconscious mind is only a repository of hurts, hang-ups, successes, habits, impulses, and every experience ever encountered or learned. It will only be awakened or revealed when probed or poked to uncover its contents, but principally, it is exercised instinctively. For instance, riding a bicycle several years after learning to ride is now an act or experience in the subconscious mind. It is only initiated when you grab the bicycle's handlebars and begin to balance on your ride. You don't have to think about it.

Renowned author Jack Canfield often talks about his successes with tapping into his subconscious mind to help him excel in his endeavors, just as several others like legendary minister and author of *The Power of the Subconscious Mind*, Joseph Murphy, do. I find the references and teachings of Joseph Murphy on the topic of the subconscious mind as relevant and informatively poignant as what I have learned from Sigmund Freud's teachings. Both are fundamental, seminal sources and anecdotal references for the precepts in this book. In Joseph Murphy's book, he refers to how scientists applied the power of the subconscious mind to tap into their research and produce phenomenal feats, which laid the foundation for modern scientific discoveries.[19] If the mind can understand its significance and power to overcome any setbacks or cognitive inhibitions, it is destined to accomplish any challenges it faces. To bolster this notion of cognitive brilliance, consider the following points.

---

[19] Joseph Murphy, *The Power of the Subconscious Mind* (Mansfield Center, CT: Martino Publishing, 2011) 71.

1. The Self

Modern science has several preconceived notions and philosophical anecdotes about one's consciousness, personality, and presence of mind, which in this context, I call the self. Teachings by renowned psychologists like Sigmund Freud or Joseph Murphy are relevant to understanding ourselves and what makes us self-aware. They are beyond the scope of the current narrative. Therefore, when I mention the self in this context, I am referring to the whole state of your cognitive awareness of desires, presence of mind, or state of consciousness in a particular space of time. Murphy discussed how Nikola Tesla, the famous electrical scientist, dwelt tirelessly on his thoughts and imaginations until he could materialize their concepts because he pulled them from his subconscious to the conscious. He also refers to how Dr. Frederick Banting, a Canadian physician and surgeon, gave time and contemplation to his thoughts on diabetes until he discovered the remedy after sleeping it over. In either case, Murphy's reference to the subconscious mind and its ability to receive insights into things that we contemplate spells a strong urge to give considerable time and effort to developing who we are (the self) so that we can address through the subconscious things we care about. Therefore, this self is the seat of all our consciousness and awareness of who we are. We are able to make sound decisions and take appropriate actions to stay who we are or become who we want to become.

2. The Mind

Our minds are complex factories of inexplicable and unsurmountable sources of cognitive brilliance and resilience. It forms a psychological phenomenon of interactions between who we are and what we want to become if we are discontent with who we see in the mirror. Psychologists and psychiatrists like Sigmund Freud and Carl Jung, respectively, have already broken the code of cognitive influence. I will not insult your intellect here by rehashing their notions or rehearsing their relevance to this narrative. However, what theories and concepts we employ and how we employ them makes the difference between who and what we become. When we take action on what we believe about ourselves, whether positively or negatively, it becomes part of our belief systems, which shape our beings. This is where the mind takes control of what we become. Our successes or failures all start from the mind. Therefore, this is probably the most important faculty or area of critical importance that we need to address in any discussion regarding how we employ the mind to manage our desires and objectives.

I would be remiss not to mention the notion of autosuggestion, which Napoleon Hill discusses. The autosuggestion phenomenon, which is medically defined by the *Merriam-Webster Dictionary* as "an influencing of one's own attitudes, behavior, or physical condition by mental processes other than conscious thought" is true as it relates to self-hypnosis. Emile Coue, a French psychologist and pharmacist, discussed this phenomenon to raise awareness of this notion in his excerpt of *Self Mastery through Conscious Autosuggestion*—a remarkable perspective on the power of the conscious and unconscious minds we all possess.[20] In understanding our subconscious, auto-suggested thoughts can form the fabric of our cognitive cloth, which wraps around our minds to prevent us from excelling beyond the status quo. Given that knowledge, understanding how to employ our auto-suggested state to our benefit is a step closer to winning any cognitive battle we may have.

---

[20]   Emile Coue, Self-Mastery through Conscious Autosuggestion, 1922, retrieved from *https://www.devonharris.com/wp-content/uploads/2019/09/self_mastery_autosuggestion_coue.pdf.*

Understanding and suggesting to the mind what it should do, believe, or avoid is critical and almost imperative to raise one's level of cognitive awareness from the subconscious mind. A week ago, I was watching a game show when the show's host asked one of the players to introduce and say something peculiar or unique about herself. The contestant described how she would wake up in the middle of her sleep, do several things, and then get back into bed. The host and some audience members exclaimed with awe that it was such a remarkable feat. This sleep-disorder behavior is commonly represented as parasomnia, also known as sleepwalking. It occurs predominantly during the non-REM (random eye movement) stage of sleep among 29 percent of children and only 4 percent of adults[21].

Interestingly, one of the remedies or therapies recommended for combating this disorder is cognitive behavioral therapy-insomnia (CBT-I). According to the excerpt, it is a therapy intended to alter, suppress, or transform negative thoughts or actions. The nature of the therapy implies an attempt to change one's auto-suggested state and condition. The relational point and relevance to this discussion on our subconscious is the suggestion that the mind is a complex and often misunderstood faculty that is so powerful in its authority to alter an entire course of life yet so vulnerable to little impulses that stimulate action. A firm grasp of how the mind works and responds to stimuli is a strong handle on conquering oneself in word or deed or helping others conquer themselves.

Now you know about the power of the subconscious mind's ability to control or direct your actions by stimuli that it has received from all sources to form a mental blueprint in your mind. You cannot help but be aware and intentional of what you let into your mind or actions because your mind tells you to. Having that sixth sense, the bridge between the self and the mind, will almost always give

---

[21]   https://www.sleepfoundation.org/parasomnias/sleepwalking.

you the desired result based on sound reasoning and judgment, contemplated review of cause and effect of the intended action, and a holistic approach to executing objectives for desired outcomes. Intuitive perception that is shaped by those mentioned earlier is the key to knowing, listening, understanding, perceiving, and deciding on what may be otherwise not readily apparent or seemingly unseen and unheard of to the eye and ear. The sixth sense is the key to unlocking the door of opportunity as you go through the gate to a world filled with unknown and unprecedented circumstances, which only a sound mind and self can overcome.

CHAPTER 5

How Is Behavior Connected to the Subconscious Mind?

If you only have a hammer, you tend
to see every problem as a nail.

—Abraham Maslow
(American psychoanalyst)

IN KINDERGARTEN, I remember getting out of my seat in the middle of a lesson, walking past a couple of desks, and stepping on another student and his desk to reach a windowsill to open the louvers. I guess I wanted to see what was happening outside. This incident led to a short brawl with the student I had just accidentally stepped on.

The result wasn't pleasant; there was blood on the other student's head. This behavior was not the first time I had disturbed the class in session. According to my mother, my teacher described my behavior in class on my report cards by two adjectives: cantankerous and boisterous. Those are some big words to describe a kid who barely knew how to spell his name correctly or when to listen to sit down attentively in class. Yet when my mother shared that story with me, I could not help but chuckle and ponder. I wondered whether I had behavioral problems because I was bored and unchallenged or external stimuli affected my sense of self and freedom of being, even at that tender age. What was occurring was a series of inexplicable thought conditions subdued in the subconscious mind, which only emerged in action when stimulated.

How we lead ourselves and behave as adults, business and organizational leaders, or parents has a lot to do with what is happening around us, what has happened to us in the past, how we have processed the thoughts we've nurtured, and what has settled deep down in our subconscious minds. Such conditions are partly why people say seemingly offensive or not politically correct things when they don't mean to say them. There is a plethora of research to prove that. After all, a scriptural passage suggests that out of the abundance of a person's heart, the mouth will speak. But how do you overcome behavior with mindset as a person, as a leader, or as a conscious and aware being? We know what behavior is, but in this writing, it is important to clarify mindset as a frame of thought in a set of belief systems that we practice. In essence, mindset drives action for one to be successful. I will uncover this notion from two perspectives.

1. Self-knowledge
2. Acceptance of mind, matter, and merit

SELF-KNOWLEDGE

Some define self-knowledge as knowledge of one's mental states, such as experiences, thoughts, and beliefs.[22] Though one's measure of self-awareness constitutes that knowledge, it is not the principal premise of discussion in the context to enhance one's consciousness. When you come to terms with who you are or what you have become, you know your triggers and tolerance that lead you to take specific courses of action. Unfortunately, several never really get past who they are in terms of the circumstances that shape their conduct, constitute their belief systems, or account for the actions they take at specified times. On some occasions while incarcerated, Nelson Mandela, former civil rights leader and first democratically elected president of the Republic of South Africa, would go on a hunger strike fueled by support from several within and outside the confines of the prison on Robben Island.[23] The guards would bring him food, and he would look at it and refuse to eat to protest the racially motivated segregation of food conditions and distribution.[24] It took an understanding of what drove passion, his physical condition, his emotional state of mind, and more importantly, how far he was willing to go to support or stand up for what he believed. Nelson Mandela epitomized that strong mental attitude and resilience that was required because he knew and understood himself.

The examples previously suggested that self-knowledge also involves how much one knows of oneself in relation to how other factors, such as relationships, influence or impact one's psyche. The idea that one can be exceptional at one's job or area of proficiency by

[22]   Brie Gertler, *Self-Knowledge* (Routledge: 2010).

[23]   Nelson Mandela, *Long Walk to Freedom: The Autobiography of Nelson Mandela* (Boston: Little, Brown, 1994).

[24]   https://blogs.scientificamerican.com/food-matters/nelson-mandelae 28099s-long-and-hungered-walk-to-freedom/.

being introverted and aloof from social or relationship building is questionable at best and unhealthy at worst. You must be prepared to develop meaningful and strategic relationships, which not only build you up but that position you to be able to overcome any cognitive, relational, or social obstacles that stand between you and your success.

During the 2020 Summer Olympics in Tokyo in 2021, the number-one gymnast and holder of multiple gold medals, Simone Byles, decided to pull out of some of the events due to her mental-health condition. As you can imagine, this decision rocked international news, especially in the United States. How could someone who was so exceptionally talented and the icon of the United States and practically the world of gymnastics do such a thing? Couldn't she just suck it up? That was the attitude of several critics. Yet one thing was certain. Simone demonstrated not only leadership and self-knowledge but also integrity and foresight. She knew her limits and understood that the mind controls the entire body, no matter how exceptional of a physical condition you might be in. Secondly, she understood that to step up, sometimes you must step down—from a position of strength by humility so that you can preserve the integrity and reputation of your essence or merit. She could see that she had a troubled mental state at the time, which would be dangerous to ignore and essentially selfish to press through with, for the risk of jeopardizing not only her health, body, and mind but also the pride and joy of the United States' performance in the Olympic games that year. This selfless act by the gymnast demonstrated a classic example of understanding one's self and mind to overcome behavior with mindset.

ACCEPTANCE OF MIND, MATTER, AND MERIT (3M)

Understanding one's mindset or self is one thing but accepting it without wallowing in a state of denial is another thing altogether.

Admitting what one thinks and how one thinks to shape actions is a sign of strength and confidence and a measure of how well one can and has overcome behavior with the mind. Acceptance of any condition beyond one's control is a powerful demonstration of strength and an important catalyst to overcoming any situation (matter) or state of significance (merit) so that one can become the best version of oneself.

Consider for a moment that you struggle with self-confidence, which is evident in your refusal to speak in public, your negative self-talk, and worse yet, your acceptance of what others think or say of you as the truth of your identity. How will you overcome any stigma someone levies on you if you don't refuse, respond, or reject it vehemently? If you accept it, it becomes your identity because that is what and how you will be known. You failed to command who you are by standing up against something that does not represent you. By first understanding who you are and what you are capable of accomplishing, you have conquered the first step to overcoming the problem of the lack of self-confidence. Consequently, accepting one's mind, matter, and merit (3M) are all part and parcel of taking the bold and important steps toward excelling in anything and everything one desires to accomplish in life. It all starts with the acceptance of one's state.

Accepting a matter is simple but challenging in some respects. In psychology, discipline is referred to as acceptance or the state of coming to terms with conditions beyond one's locus of control. However, in socio-economic terms, one must resolve to accept circumstances surrounding relationships with others and means of sustenance if one has exhausted all avenues or efforts to control or take charge of one's future. In the 1960s, Sir Stephen Hawking, the renowned theoretical physicist, contracted a debilitating amyotrophic lateral sclerosis disease. This illness subdued his muscular systems and extremities, and it limited the extent of his motor functions.[25] Hawking went on to become the Center for Theoretical Cosmology research leader and director for his alma mater at the University of Cambridge before passing away in March of 2018. Hawking's contribution to humanity in theoretical physics is well documented and researched. In this reference to Hawking, one surmises that he had to accept his condition in his mind as permanently limiting his physical mobility. Secondly, he had to accept the daily limitations that he experienced as the reality of the matter. Thirdly and ultimately, he had to accept the fact that none of those circumstances of his condition changed the merit of who he was or what he was capable of doing with his mind, but only what he desired to do with his extremities or mobility that his condition would not allow. This three-pronged approach of acceptance as part of the subconscious-behavior-mapping paradigm is a fundamental premise to aid in progressing through overcoming behavior with the mind.

TYING SELF-KNOWLEDGE WITH 3M

If you had told me in my teenage years that whatever I said or thought reflected who I was and what I believed was evidenced in action, I would have suggested that I could control my actions apart from my thoughts. In essence, I could believe one way—let's say party all night and not study while in college (mindset) and wake up the next morning and take a test (action) expecting to pass. Except in a few exceptional cases, it is essentially impossible to have little chance of passing a test if you have not studied the material well enough to abandon it the night before. The knowledge of how smart one is on the material for a test will determine how much time, effort, and risk of not studying one has to take. Therefore, if one believes

---

[25]   *https://www.britannica.com/biography/Stephen-Hawking.*

(mindset) that the test is easy to pass (matter), one will preserve one's smartness (merit) by not studying and blowing off any preparation by partying—a classic case of behavior and subconscious mapping for a college student.

As you know, in almost all cases, few can pull that off. Those who are successful at not preparing adequately for anything and yet doing very well at it may have precociously mastered their self-knowledge and strengths and adequately aligned their 3M to meet their desired objectives for success. They will always leverage this self-knowledge and understanding of the 3M paradigm to excel in life. Most don't have that intuitive self-knowledge, and they must be coached through it. This alignment of self-knowledge and 3M lies at the crux of mapping our conscious behaviors with our subconscious thoughts or subdued impressions of our conduct to enable us to increase our self-awareness and decrease our inhibiting mindsets. Figure I below illustrates this paradigm. It suggests that one's enhanced self-awareness is evident in behavior because of the mastery of a well-aligned 3M self-knowledge and subconscious.

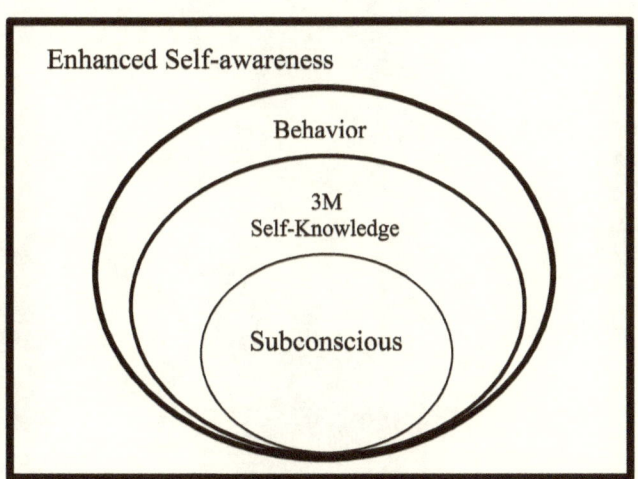

Figure I. Behavior-Subconscious Mapping
to Enhance Self-Awareness

When one comprehends and masters the 3M self-knowledge paradigm, the coaching process becomes a little smoother because the coach puts into perspective the interrelationships among notions buried in the subconscious mind and revealed in behavior. Ultimately, leaders enhance their self-awareness with the assistance of a coach when they embrace this paradigm well.

CHAPTER 6

What Your Unconscious Mind Reveals about Leading from the Inside

Before something can become a habit it
must first be practiced as a discipline.

—Ken Blanchard (American author)

WHEN A LEADER leads from the inside, that leader leads from a
self-will position, which could be a skewed or unchallenged perspective. The leader has no external critical stimulus that interrogates
questionable judgment or objection to actions. In this state, the leader
has a guard, block, or mechanism that precludes crucial objection
or forceful backup to decision-making. Some of these could be an
absence of a feedback loop for customers, no accountability partner,
no person to verify actions, no board of directors to weigh decisions,

or no opportunity to reflect on the results of executed decisions. The leader leads from the inside when his or her behavior is unfiltered and ruled by the unconscious mind and based on past hurts and hang-ups from the subconscious. The leader's behaviors are based only on how that leader perceives actions from his or her perspective, and it is short of what others perceive. This is an approach akin to Swiss psychologist Jean Piaget's psychological explanation of egocentrism, which suggests one's inability to see the self-centered nature of one's notion while ignoring the subjective perceptions of others within the same context of time and space.[26]

LEADERSHIP MYOPIA

Leadership myopia typically refers to the near or shortsightedness of leaders who fail to see the projected outcomes or visionary impacts of their decision-making. In the context of this book, the perceptive leadership approach of leadership myopia is a paradigm that predicates a *What's in it for me?* attitude, which creates an air of egocentrism and task-driven objectivity at the expense of people-oriented subjectivity. The leader always focuses only on the desired objective and agenda to a fault, which blinds him or her from the impact it creates on those who must execute that leader's vision. Have you ever come across someone like that? Everything is about getting the job done to show what the leader is capable of doing. Does anyone know somebody like that? This tendency may be what some call cognitive myopia, a psychological behavior that limits one from taking present actions already existent or evident for one's own preconceived notions.[27] The leader has blinders on to

---

[26]   *https://www.britannica.com/science/egocentrism.*

[27]   E. Weber, "Breaking Cognitive Barriers to a Sustainable Future," Natural Human Behavior, 2017, 1, 0013, *https://doi.org/10.1038/s41562-016-0013.*

what goes on with followers because the overwhelming obsession within is to accomplish a task, objective, evolution, or dream, which has been a lifelong preoccupation. A leader with this approach will do almost anything passionately, if not everything, at any expense to accomplish a desired objective. Though this passion may be essential for success, it is detrimental to leadership, self, and certainly any social environment where one must relate to others. It is an internal battle that a strong paradigm shift in one's mental presence of mind and operational environment must overcome.

A leader who never gets past leadership from the inside—that is, leading by a paradigm or philosophy that is self-willed and over time ill-fated—is a detriment to self and society. Because the leader does not recognize the impact of actions or circumstances, the leader consequently creates an incessant, overpowering aura that becomes normalized and accepted as a natural condition of circumstance. This ultimately becomes the leader's demise, along with those affected by that leadership. In 1933, Adolf Hitler became the leader of Germany. Over time, his troubled past and questionable leadership led to the death of over eleven million Europeans, six million of whom were Jews who died for no reason at all, except what was ill-conceived in the mind of Hitler.[28] Accounts of how this leader thought and translated his thoughts into action are well-documented across a plethora of literature, which are beyond the scope of this book. However, it establishes a poignant reference to the caliber of a person who does not grow, lead, or overcome this cognitive stronghold. Leading from the inside suggests that leadership actions are exclusively autonomous and are irrespective of any other external or perceptually critical notion. Usually, as alluded, this is typically authoritarian, dictatorial, or in some cases, just autocratic, and it fails human relations and welfare with a standard humane protocols test.

---

[28]   https://www.biography.com/dictator/adolf-hitler.

THE STATE OF A SUBCONSCIOUS MIND

To fully appreciate where one's subconscious mind is, one must think of elementary or high school science class, where one is taught to think of an atom as the smallest particle of a substance called matter. Matter is anything that is palpable or that can occupy space, correct? An atom is visible under a microscope and roams freely until another one is present to bond with to form a molecule. Well, one can liken the space that the atom resides in until it bonds with another as the subconscious mind—a place where small or in some cases, big individually conceived or acquired pieces of ideas, thoughts, or anything that one allows to enter one's mind resides.

Subconscious thoughts or notions will remain in this random, free-roaming state until called upon to perform or be recognized. The subconscious mind is always deeply seated in all the circumstances we have ever encountered, whether knowingly or unwittingly, including those that may be potentially emotionally damaging to ourselves. The subconscious mind is often part of the mind that is suppressed, regressed, and not readily accessible until stimulated. Often, this stimulation or trigger is initiated by the unconscious mind. The unconscious mind is the involuntary agitator or initiator of our subconscious conditions, which desire recognition or action.

For the subconscious mind—every thought, impression, desire, perception, or emotion—is buried deep down in the mind's abyss and is ready to be awakened when the conditions are just right, and the unconscious mind triggers it. Therefore, one must understand the state of the subconscious mind as a mental disposition. It cannot and should not be left unresolved or unsettled on any potential mentally or emotionally traumatic notions that may subsequently become detrimental to the mental health of the person. It is imperative to resolve it early and often, especially for the executive leader.

THE STATE OF AN UNCONSCIOUS MIND

An unconscious mind is one that triggers spontaneous action from the subconscious mind. This state of mind is where actions or behaviors emerge that are unintended or premature. Think of an unconscious mind as the performer of the subconscious mind. Whatever triggers the unconscious mind will automatically reach back into the depth of the subconscious mind to retrieve the desired or expected response requested by the unconscious mind for performance. An example of this kind of behavior is what some attribute to the Freudian slip when someone says something unintentionally. In the context of this narrative, the unconscious mind is always ready to enact anything that lurks or that is deeply buried in the subconscious mind, if the conditions are right or the stimulation of thought is ideal to trigger an unconscious act or behavior. A typical example alluded to is the tendency for people to say things they don't really mean. How often haven't you heard people say, "What I meant to say was." A typical reference to such incidents were quite evident and well-documented across several medias on how the former president of the United States Donald Trump said several things that were deemed controversial, insensitive, or blatantly erroneous and that never fell short of inciting conversations across dinner tables or media outlets. However, it was evident that he was clearly articulating whatever he felt or whatever lurked in his mind at the time. Why would someone not say exactly what he or she wants to say and allow some unintended utterance to occur? The fact is that the human mind has an unconscious mind, which one has no control over because it instigates our thoughts, perceptions, deepest desires, or pleasures unwittingly through actions. Just as breathing occurs unconsciously without thinking about it or making a mentally conscious effort, deeply suppressed thoughts, impressions, reservations, or desires also show up in speech and behavior without the intention to because they are unconsciously expressed.

The unconscious mind is, therefore, the most significant evidence of our unintentional behaviors. For this reason, we must consciously and unequivocally determine to address every subconsciously held notion or premise about our lives by intentionally trying to filter them and receiving professional counseling, coaching, direction, education, or therapy to unearth or settle them. Settling the mental perceptions or impressions in our minds means coming to terms with whether they are positive for our well-being or are inherently dangerous and ill-fated for our success. Scientific research over several decades proves that any suppressed emotional or mental trauma that occurs early in childhood and sometimes even in adulthood can be devastating to an individual later on in life, due to the circumstances that trigger the trauma resurfacing or occurring in a present state. Therefore, bad, unresolved situations are never left without a favorable situation or outcome.

THE LINK: SUBCONSCIOUS TO UNCONSCIOUS

With the knowledge and understanding of the state of both subconscious and unconscious behaviors, it is essential to mention that a leader who does not address any subconsciously suppressed or reserved notions of the past is likely to incur some unintentional behaviors. For instance, it is not uncommon for political figures running in a political race to say things that appear racially insensitive or politically incorrect by the decorum of the society in which they spoke. These statements that may have been said unconsciously compel an apology or a reframing by another political figure, aide, or the same person, who attempts to perform damage control on the statement and to smooth it by statements like, "What I meant to say was," or "What he was saying was." When one learns to master the health of the subconscious mind, the unconscious mind revealed in behavior is almost always an unscathed expression of thoughts and intents with full self-awareness. However, when leaders lead from the inside—that is, from the subconscious alone without processed, settled, or coached cognitive filters—they lead by instinct, unconscious trauma, and in some cases, harbored prejudices, which result in significant social-political and even personal problems in the future.

In 2017, the world learned that Martin Shkreli, a pharmaceutical company's former chief executive officer, was convicted of hiking a lifesaving drug price by 5,000 percent. Yet as of 2021, he continued to exert influence in his organization by being able to vote on shares while incarcerated.[29] He gave new meaning to leading from the inside. However, I would argue that besides a broken system, which allows that to transpire, his blatant defiance of ethical judgment or lack of awareness and its impact on social and professional relationships remain troubling at the very least. Clearly, the link between his subconscious and unconscious mind was flawed enough to compel unprocessed or unfiltered actions. This kind of behavior conceived and perpetuated within one's mind at the expense and disregard of the social, professional, or environmental ramifications is what the Triple C leadership coaching method seeks to resolve as it moves leaders into successful leadership practices. When you are fully aware of your influence over others and that your conduct, decision-making, and direction to others for action can spell significant impacts, the need to exercise leadership from the subconscious through the conscious becomes imperative for success.

---

29   Michael J. de la Merced, The New York Times, July 9, 2021, retrieved from *https://www.nytimes.com/2021/07/09/business/dealbook/martin-shkreli-pharma-control.html?.?mc=aud_dev&ad-keywords=auddevgate&gclid=CjwK CAjw4qCKBhAVEiwAkTYsPKPZqoW3ppyrUfwe-Dqqzn9yl6yNtcSPoAkj_ Sn5iEMHhfrCMbjQsRoCy_gQAvD_BwE&gclsrc=aw.ds.*

To establish the link between the unconscious and the sub-conscious mind, the leader must be in a comfortable state, which elicits an inner search for the most concerning or deeply rooted experiences that manifest in unannounced or unwelcome action. A leader's wellness in mind, spirit (social), and body consequently rests with how much of an extrinsic influence (stimulus) the leader has received, which compels an intrinsic response (conscious) to get better and do better. It means that for a leader to do well or desire to be well, that leader must allow all subconscious thoughts or dispositions that manifest unconsciously to be overcome through coaching. The leader should be coachable and responsive enough to the measure of critique or accountability that will enhance performance. Coaching a leader to the gap that is evident takes humility from that leader to be vulnerable and willing. Therefore, every effort to get healthy and well will depend on the intrinsic motivators, which have a deep well of personal pride and spirit of excellence to draw from. As a leadership health and wellness coach, your role is vital in eliciting and probing challenging thoughts to enable your client to become a leader who is well enough to lead to his or her fullest measure. Some key strategic coaching elements to elicit dialogue and thoughts from the client are

- Always ask permission from the client to start each session with a mindful moment. It helps that individual relax the mind and de-stress from the day.
- Always be present in the moment with the client by leaning into his or her feelings and thoughts as that person expresses himself or herself so that being empathetic will only come naturally.
- Always reflect on (paraphrase back) the client's statements to ensure that he or she is right. It builds trust and confidence that you are attentive and in tune with every word he or she says.

- Always be ready to adjust to the client's shift in focus as that individual draws out deeply rooted thoughts or concerns from his or her subconscious to the forefront of the dialogue.

Overall, allowing the link between the unconscious and subconscious mind to be free and uninhibited of expression requires the right environment and setting, which is free of judgment, deprivation, or objection. This is why mindfulness and presence are essential elements of the coaching process to attain the best results from the Triple C process.

CHAPTER 7

What Your Conscious Mind Tells You about Leading from the Inside-Out

A life lived of choice is a life of conscious action.
A life lived of chance is a life of unconscious creation.

—Neale Donald Walsh
(American author and actor)

WHEN ONE LEADS from the inside out, it means one who leads from a position of introspection and actionable foresight based on what one's thoughts or impressions are (inside) and what is occurring in the environment that may impact one's life (out). Too often, leaders are not only reactive and self-serving, but they can also be indifferent or insensitive to life around them because they may be far removed from day-to-day operations. In recent years, the need for cultural awareness, sensitivity training of supervisors and managers, diversity, equity, and inclusion training in organizations have become essential to enable leaders to perform at their peaks. Leading from the inside out allows one to consciously and proactively foster a cohesive and collaborative work or social environment where one applies cognitive filters or processed applications to thoughts, impressions, or emotions, as well as utterances and behaviors.

Many attribute exceptional and amiable leadership to the fortieth president of the United States, President Ronald Wilson Reagan, because of his excellent communication prowess and influence in helping to bring down the communist wall of the Soviet Union. This influence partly resulted from his self-awareness of the circumstances around him and the impacts of what he said to others. Several of his life's accomplishments made him likable and competently compelling until he succumbed to his health later in his years. The point here is that when one employs one's mental state toward seeing how to relate and improve circumstances around one's life, the focus of effort and state of mind shift from self-focused to others focused. This state of mind consequently facilitates a consciousness that hardly, if at all, taps into the subconscious mind.

A SUBCONSCIOUS THROUGH CONSCIOUS MINDSET

The notion that one is fully aware of one's behavioral shortcomings or blind spots when elderly or seasoned in a particular role or place of authority is inaccurate and nonsensical. Well into the fourth quarter of their adult lives, several leaders have sounded and behaved very immaturely because they have either been deprived of a self-awareness mechanism or a nurturing environment that enhances introspection and critical feedback. This situation may have occurred either intentionally or unintentionally. However, regardless of the circumstances, the inability to have or create a mindset founded on introspective behavior and influential conduct is a problem that merits resolving.

A subconscious through conscious mindset means a state of self-awareness that accounts for adequate processing of sub-consciously held perceptions or emotions in conscious behavior. This behavior yields positive and productive social or professional results. This means one has full control of one's cognitive faculties, regardless of what circumstances occur outside one's locus of control or environment.

One is fully aware of intrinsic limitations when leading from a state of consciousness. These may be thoughts, emotions, perceptions, and prejudices harbored in the subconscious mind but adjudicated or filtered through a preconscious mindset with facts or realities that influence decision-making. For instance, a department store manager who may have experienced a history of psychologically traumatic sexual harassment or assault may harbor this indelible mental situation in the subconscious mind. Knowing how such trauma can influence others makes the manager sensitive to mannerisms or innuendos that suggest sexual connotations. Therefore, the manager's defenses and discipline of self-mastery control desired responsive behavior whenever anyone demonstrates behaviors akin to the previously experienced negative behaviors. The manager responds verbally or behaviorally with caution and consideration not to allow the past trauma to taint the present circumstance. This decision occurs in a preconscious state of mind, which requires full awareness of the environmental circumstances in which a situation unfolds. Consequently, the manager either makes a statement to disrupt or dissuade the undesirable indications of sexual misbehavior. Alternatively, the manager may behave in a pleasant, tolerant, accommodating, rational, or responsive manner by walking away or physically disapproving or denouncing the threatening situation to prevent it from recurring.

This process of active behavior, which started in the subconscious mind, ultimately shows up in the conscious mind through active demonstration of the displeasure. The department store manager would have effectively led from the inside out by enabling a process that activates the subconscious mind to consider present circumstances, determining the relevance or viability of a situation using various interpersonal skills, and then actively allowing the situation to manifest in a controlled or vetted occurrence.

SOUND CONSCIOUS BEHAVIOR

Though I have covered this leader in previous sections, I refer to him again in this context because it is fitting. From 1964 to 1982, when Nelson Mandela was incarcerated at Robben Island in South Africa as a political prisoner, harsh conditions that could easily break anyone's psychological or mental state did not consume him. Instead, he prevailed through hunger strikes and mentally challenging circumstances[30]. As previously mentioned, some of these were deplorable living and eating conditions that were humanely displeasing. Offers of political compromise in exchange for release from prison presented to Mandela on several occasions were enticing. Still, he refused them in protest for freedom and equality for the natives of South Africa. With persistence and solid mental conditioning, he was released from prison, and consequently, he became the first democratically elected president of South Africa in 1994. He ruled for one term. He left the office with a sound mind, which had experienced immeasurable trauma and disappointments on several accounts and at different levels. The history of South

---

[30]   *https://www.britannica.com/biography/Nelson-Mandela.*

African resistance and the fight against the apartheid regime are widely documented, and they reveal the grit of Nelson Mandela. His ability to withstand the challenges of his past and effectively sustain his cognitive ability to lead a nation even in his advanced age suggested one who had overcome his past, understood his present, and adequately prepared and built upon his past experiences to enhance his future. He epitomized one who led from the inside out. He never allowed his past circumstances to undermine his present state and jeopardize his future desires.

To have a sound mind, one must have a strong moral, ethical, and spiritual compass, which gives direction and purpose to one's livelihood. One must exercise control of one's mind by any means and methods to enable personal and professional growth. Just as Joseph Murphy teaches how to control the mind, so do these steps to success, which lead to a sound mind.

1. Identify what truly makes you happiest when you do it. In essence, it's what you like doing best on this planet and endeavoring to do exactly that. If you don't know what it is, do a deep soul search to discover what you are passionately in love with doing on this earth. This discovery is the beginning of having your clarity of mind and being yourself.

2. Secondly, once you find this passionate obsession, specialize in an aspect of it. If it is basket weaving, well, be the best fishing basket, shopping basket, or even picnic basket weaver ever. When you identify this specialty area, you become the resident expert or go-to person because you love it, and you have placed an aspect of this passion that you are the best at. A well-placed self-discovery enables you to have a confident mind, which is clear on its objectives and exceptional in its purpose and delivery to humanity.

3. The passion you possess for this vocation or obsession does not bring only success but also changes the lives of others and makes them successful too. This altruistic tendency is what seals the deal for having a sound mind when one knows that it is more blessed to give than to receive and that someone else is happier because one has made a difference in his or her life. One's spirit is encouraged and enriched because one feels a sense of fulfillment guaranteed.

LEADING FROM THE INSIDE OUT

When Earl Nightingale said that success is the progressive realization of a worthy goal or ideal, he was in essence, referring to how one attains success within one's own definition of what success looks like. It is never a measure of what others perceive success to be for that individual. Suppose I decide to wake up at 9:00 a.m. every day to get ready for work and arrive at work by 11:00 a.m. In that case, my day's work is completed by 3:00 p.m. It brings me the transformational and worthy result I desire. I have essentially attained the measure of success I desire. However, very little if any can or could be accomplished with such a schedule, but it does not dismiss what success looks like for me. Clarity of purpose and pursuit of an ideal bring drive and value to your mind and make you effective when leading from the inside out.

With this illustration of what a sound mind reveals or entails, one's behavior must be evident in light of one who knows what one is passionate about and pursues it. Evidence of a sound mind should occur so one can give and reach back to add value to others. This behavior may be unquestionably altruistic, selfless, benevolent, philanthropic, and in most cases, repetitive and incessant. When you as a leader can relate to this state of mind and rehearse it boldly and without reservation in your own life, you can begin to confess and confirm that you have indeed led or are leading from your subconscious through to your conscious ideals. Leaders need to aspire to this state of mind when their subconscious minds do not rule their conscious, but rather, their actions and presence of mind are in full control to reveal their desired actions toward that worthy ideal they desire to attain.

So what happens when you as a leader cannot work through cognitive challenges that give you pursuit of your goals and desires? You will need someone to challenge your perspectives and objectives to reach that goal. You cannot be objective when the aforementioned ideals or steps are questionable.

To fully leverage the power of absolute mastery or control of the subconscious mind so that you can manifest consciously in your behavior, you must consider what Joseph Murphy refers to as the law of belief. He suggests that belief is a state of mind that allows what you have in your subconscious mind to permeate every aspect of your life by the thought patterns or habits you exercise. These principles are the law that all world religions are founded on. The same principles of belief you have about any faith or paradigm will drive your actions to act as a blueprint for your cognitive success. He reminds that this is the principle that so-called traditional, blind faith healers exploit to bring healing to those who believe in it, such as the Swiss physician Anton Mesmer. An account of the physician in 1776 claims healing through magnets to create a magnetic field, which transferred fluid from him to the bodies of stroked, diseased patients who came to him in droves. When the Academy of Science launched an investigation, they uncovered no evidence except that it was all the patients' perceptions. The result was a clear case of how belief can transform behavior and action in the lives of those who exercise it.

This powerful cognitive principle of belief aims to bring transformational change to those who exercise it faithfully. All leaders must strive to exercise this and where unable to, seek professional help to uncover and understand the processes and strategies required to excel and be at their peak performances. Understanding the principles and tenets of the cognitive approach to leadership coaching unearths the core of our greatest fears. It helps us work through those fears to make what we perceive as our greatest fantasies a definite reality in our world.

CHAPTER 8

How to Employ the Connected Cognitive Coaching (Triple C) Model

Self-belief does not necessarily ensure success,
but self-disbelief assuredly spawns failure.

—Albert Bandura
(Canadian American psychologist)

WHEN I FIRST began to understand the power of a conscious mind and its impact on my behavior, I was young, naïve, and seemingly oblivious to the notion that how I did one thing was how I did everything. I was sitting on the steps of my dormitory, wondering how I would navigate this responsibility as the student in charge of ensuring the well-being of the students in my charge. I claimed responsibility for anything and everything that would make their lives on campus a success. It was my job and therefore, my responsibility to see them all live in a home away from home. After all, it was a boarding school. I was unprepared for what would happen next.

THE GENESIS

At about 5:00 a.m., I awoke to some commotion that needed my attention. Somehow, a student had been kicked out of his dorm room because he was gay. Now, this was well before the age and movements of diversity, equity, and inclusion. This was an era where sexual preferences were never discussed. They were considered taboo in any circle. I had to make sure that this student found a place to stay. I had to give up my own room, which was semi-detached from the rest of the dormitories. A room designated only for the dormitory adjutant—sometimes referred to as the residence assistant—was considered the best room of its kind. I did this against my own inherent biases and notions about sexual orientations or preferences at the time.

You would probably argue that I didn't have to do that. I could have shared the room with him, found another way to resolve the situation, or another brilliant option you can conceive of besides the action I took. It's your prerogative to question my decision or approach. That outcome was the reality at the time. You might ask why I took that action or step. Well, I quickly learned that as a leader, I had to overcome my own preconceived notions, impressions, limiting beliefs, or personal reservations for the sake of leading well so that others could live well. This was the beginning of my renaissance into self-realization, cognitive or subconscious maturity, and performance. I began to learn how to allow my subconscious thoughts and self-limiting beliefs to filter through my knowledge and experiential base of a network of realistic stimuli. Everything around me was not based on what I thought, felt, or expected it to be just because that was what I had always known, had always been, or expected it to be. A pragmatic leader considers his or her life's values or governing ethos and relates it to the reality of the environment in which that leader lives. When this occurs, any of these three things will or should happen.

1. The leader accepts the circumstance or environment as reality and takes no action to alter it.
2. The leader denies the reality of the circumstance occurring in the environment with the hope that it will change on its own.
3. The leader develops a system, process, or action that influences or changes the reality occurring in the considered environment.

To aid the leader in taking action and discovering the areas of his or her life that are burdened, as the coach, it is incumbent upon you to help that leader narrow down the stimulating factors that inhibit performance or create cognitive ambivalence. Which aspects of the client's life are not balanced with his or her goals? For this reason, I recommend employing the Leadership Wheel of Balance tool (Figure 2 below) I developed to assess and discover which aspects of the leader's life exert the most pressure, scored from 0 to 10.

LEADERSHIP WHEEL OF BALANCE

The Leadership Wheel of Balance tool is not an originally new coaching model or concept. Other coaching professionals have employed variations of the model to align areas of concern to priorities of effort for coaching. Before delving into the Leadership Wheel of Balance, it is important to address Albert Bandura's social cognitive theory, which emphasizes one's behaviors or living in relation to one's social stimuli, environmental stimuli, and one's own learned behaviors.[31] These behaviors compel or influence one's actions. My approach and selection of focus areas that a leader might present as concerning or worthy of addressing are modifications in this design. They break up into two sections: Professional and personal potential areas of concern, which will lead to the leader's wellness vision of sound leadership health. The following areas are pertinent to any leader. They must be thoroughly explored before the first coaching session and periodically after that to ensure that the mind remains aligned with the leader's desired goals and objectives. They must be unencumbered by less relevant distractions. They are the following.

PERSONAL SPIRITUALITY

One's spirituality often gives one a sense of central balance or serenity. Usually, this could be associated with one's state of mental health. Therefore, sound mental health denotes an optimal spirituality, where a leader finds internal peace and inspiration to excel or accomplish desired objectives. Spirituality usually refers to one's faith or personal inspiration from a place of serenity, such as yoga, tai chi, or meditation. For a Christian, sound mental health rests in the knowledge and belief in God to provide the direction and mental clarity one desires to live a wholesome, fulfilling life. In this case, one with a sound mind has the mind of Christ, as clearly articulated in the Bible that we "have the mind of Christ"[32]. When this aspect of one's mind is healthy, one will almost always have clarity of mind and objectivity as a leader, so all other aspects of one's life should fall in balance. Everything that affects all other leadership wellness

---

[31]   Albert Bandura, *Social Learning Theory* (New York, NY: General Learning Press, 1971).

[32]   *King James Version Bible*. (2017). American Bible Society (Original work published 1769).

areas hinges on this one wellness category—the mind revealed in personal spirituality.

PERSONAL GROWTH

This area of one's life begins the quest for excellence and introspection to determine whether one needs to evaluate the aspects of one's physical, social, and mental health for alignment with one's leadership objectives. Personal growth requires a desire not to settle for the status quo but to seek ways and means to increase one's expertise, aptitude, and performance so that one can be deeply attuned to personal goals and achievements.

PHYSICAL HEALTH

Physical health is one of the most challenging areas to discipline if one's personal growth and mental health (spirituality) are not well-aligned. Eating habits, sleep routines, exercise regimen, and physical abuse of varied proportions can affect the well-being of a leader. This may throw the leader off balance in attaining their desired objectives. Therefore, it is imperative to ensure that there is clarity that the leader desires to stay physically healthy. A good night's sleep is arguably one critical need for sound physical health. Therefore, if you are sleep-deprived and are stressed as a leader, you will likely be ineffective in your leadership role. Take care of your body so that it can take good care of you.

SOCIAL RELATIONSHIPS

When the leader has a clear mind of how to lead and what goals or objectives must be accomplished because he or she is rooted in a sound mental state, that person's own sense of personal balance improves. The relationships he or she forms and how that individual nurtures those relationships become a healthy consequence of the aforementioned areas of leadership health and balance.

FINANCIAL STABILITY

Any aspect of finances in one's professional life can cause undue stress. Anxiety over a desire for a higher paying job, more hours to earn more money, or how to balance earned income with life expenses can easily and negatively impact the overall well-being of the leader. Consequently, assessing how the leader perceives their current financial state is imperative.

OCCUPATIONAL CONTROL

The category of occupational control is the sense of purpose that one feels about having a career or job that earns a livelihood. The kind of fulfillment or confidence that comes with knowing that one feels secure in one's role or purposeful career reduces any anxiety or stress, mainly if it is well compensated. The contrary is also true that when one has to deal with the pressure of an unstable career, the leader in this state will be dysfunctional, and he or she will not be at his or her optimal peak to perform.

CULTURAL INFLUENCE

You cannot overstate the influence that one's culture has on one's well-being. When a leader is nurtured in an environment that may have been very conservative or fairly liberal in thought, responsibilities, or obligations, training those that he or she leads and creating a culture that works well for the organization, its people, and the clients he or she serves are critical considerations to explore.

When conflicting notions or expectations occur, these may present significant cultural implications to the leader and the organization and throw the entire team's health in disarray. Therefore, having a healthy cultural balance with a tone set by the leader is imperative to mitigate and ease any stressful anxiety that the leader might have.

GOALS ATTAINMENT

Finally, the stress of being unable to accomplish one's goals may be a clear and present concern, which might impact a leader for one reason or another. It is sometimes unclear why desired organizational goals are unmet, due to managerial shortfalls or blatant inability to sustain organizational demands. Whatever the reason, it is important that any leader of any organization meets goals and objectives to stay viable. Suppose these objectives remain unmet or challenging in any capacity, the measure of stress and anxiety resulting from such situations may certainly impact the leader's mental health and begin the cycle of cognitive implications again, where the fear of failure becomes an overbearing concern.

Overall, these eight categories are worth considering as the beginning benchmark for ascertaining a sound state of leadership health and wellness. A sound benchmark is important so that one will be well on their way to developing and sustaining a wellness vision, which is set with a leadership health and wellness coach to achieve desired results.

The figure below illustrates the respective categories in which the leader will shade from 0 in the inner circles to 10 on the outer ones. This depicts the measure of concern, anxiety, stress, or displeasure felt, if any, in those respective categories. This assessment provides the leadership health and wellness coach with a baseline from which to begin building and relating to the primary needs and concerns of the leader.

A few years ago, I had just walked through the door from a midweek service at our local church. My fingers were tired from the chill outside, my body ached from the day's work, and my throat was patched from talking all day. As I sat in my favorite seat in the living room, ready to take a deep breath, my cell phone rang. It was from one of our senior pastors. "John is dead!" he said.

I wasn't sure I heard correctly. "What do you mean he's dead?" I exclaimed.

"Yes! He shot himself!" he went on to state. At that moment, I felt fear, pain, and anger overshadow my body, which overwhelmed the already troubled state that I was in. A friend had lost his battle with mental health. He was a leader. He was a man. He took pride in his work. He was no more because no one seemed to help him overcome the stressors in his life. Mental health rules the other aspects of our livelihood, and if you, as the leadership health and wellness coach, must be impactful, you must muster the courage to see past the seen hurts and listen for the unheard heartaches of those who need your attention most.

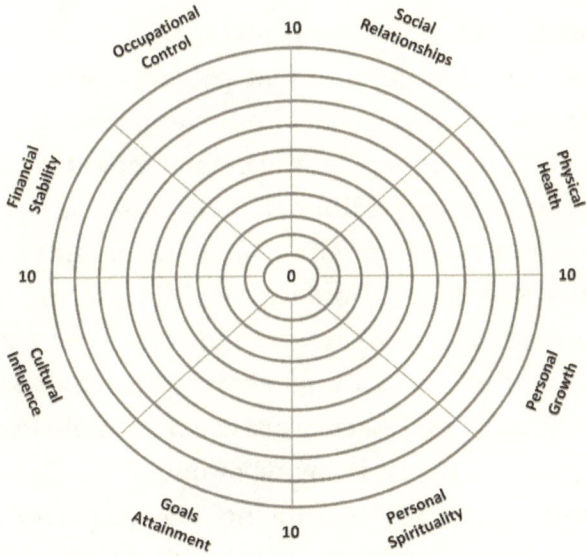

Figure 2. Leadership Wheel of Balance

Some leaders who experience cognitive dissonance fall into the temptation of fleeing a challenge they are unfamiliar with or react negatively by persistent and constant pushback or undue exercise of authority to combat, deny, or ignore the problem's existence. Others passively do nothing to influence the circumstance and yet complain, derail, or sabotage every effort that permeates. The third more proactive and practical approach reflects those who consider all aspects of the situation and take a holistic approach to influencing, modifying, or changing the reality of the situation, if and only if, it is detrimental to the organization's success. Doing so takes being clearly intentional and mindful of how to change the circumstance or environment that hinders your progress or remains an obstacle for your productivity. The cognitive approach to executive leadership coaching becomes useful when you are challenged to enact and enforce this change.

THE CONNECTED COGNITIVE APPROACH

When coaching, before any buy-in, introspection, or commitment to transformation can occur for the client, patient, or whatever term you choose to describe the one who will receive your support, you must have a rapport with that person. You cannot move forward without establishing this rapport. Additionally, you must understand exactly what that person needs; otherwise, you risk wasting your time and that individual's. A specific and thorough intake and assessment process should enable you to understand your client very well or at least partially before attempting to employ coaching strategies to attain results. Too often, coaches are eager to apply their skills or sell their expertise without knowing or understanding the client's needs or holistic state. Your "medicine" may be prescribed for the wrong ailment. Therefore, listening to the client is half the battle or challenge toward a victorious outcome.

During my earlier years of business executive leadership coaching, I once had a prospect who needed my services, so he contacted me for help. Normally, I run every business leader and his or her organization through a standardized assessment to determine what that person needs to be successful. In one case, I started to run the prospect through an assessment tool that I was confident was the ideal fit for him because everyone else who fell into that client category needed that assessment tool. Halfway through the forty-five-minute assessment, we both realized that all the questions and the impact I was seemingly creating was not what he needed—more clients and money wasn't what he needed. He needed efficiency and process transformation. I had wasted a whole hour only to arrive at a counterproductive outcome. You see, not everyone needs what seems the most obvious to us: money. That person needs you to listen to him or her carefully and read between the lines. You need to listen to what that individual is not vocalizing.

To understand how the connected cognitive approach works, consider that everyone, like you and me, harbors inherent fears based on his or her upbringing, past experiences, perceptions, or biased impressions. These *fears* reside deep in our subconscious mind. They are only activated or awakened when they are stimulated by a trigger. This trigger may be an external stimulus like a statement, an observation, a familiar situation, or a previously experienced condition. These fears, if not resolved over time, sit in our minds and remain our repressed subconscious demons or discontent. These fears must be overcome by facts. These facts should debunk, refute, or discredit the fears, whether legitimate or perceived, so that you can be effective in changing the circumstance or environment that threatens your success and productivity. Facts don't lie or misinform. They are indisputable, fundamentally sourced, and conventionally accepted as norms or premises. For instance, there will always be a period of daylight and a period of night without sunlight (unless you're at the North Pole); therefore, if you are afraid of darkness, you must understand that the cycle is never going to change. Additionally, you must recognize and know that the darkness is only an absence of photons—these are facts. If your life resolves to these facts as you harbor this fear of darkness, you will realize that the fear prevents you from being effective and that you will have to find a way to overcome it by leveraging knowledge of the fundamental truths. If going from your home to the car and driving to dinner is an unsettling chore and a challenge for you because of your inherent fear of darkness, it will prevent you from performing at your peak of impressing your date or sealing that deal. Before intervention, you would likely rationalize your fear as a dislike for night driving or discomfort with restaurants. You may even argue with others or strongly resent anything that has to do with leaving your home after dark. The real core of the reason may never be known to others. Only you will know the internal struggle you have with this fear. A connected cognitive approach to remedy this challenge is imperative.

Once you have determined the facts and fears you have and rejected the limitations that fear creates, it should be evident that your facts debunk your fears. With those facts about darkness being only the absence of photons, it becomes incumbent upon you to determine how you can apply them to attain your fantasies, whatever they may be. If you fantasize about going to dinner with your date at 7:00 p.m. when it is dark outside, yet you convince yourself that you don't like dinners or don't like driving after 6:00 or 7:00 p.m. when there is no more sunlight, the real reason has to be unearthed. Unfortunately, some leaders never get past this mental block by themselves. A connected cognitive approach will attempt to isolate the inherent, undisclosed fear from the apparent environment that triggers the fear and prevents your effectiveness. With the knowledge you have gained either through a third party or your own self-knowledge and coping mechanisms, you must find strategies, methods, and systems. These will empower you to apply those facts to enjoy your fantasies—in this case, going to dinner with your date, regardless of how dark it is outside. Often, getting to a state of mind where you are convinced that your inherent reservations have no bearing on how you feel takes time. Expressing when or why you accomplish your desired objectives takes some time and a transitional process of self-awareness and perceptive growth.

THE CONNECTED COGNITIVE TRANSITION

As a leader, everyone looks to you to stand up against your fears or challenges and take action to fulfill the mission you set out to do. This expectation implies you must understand what your inherent fears are, apply the facts related to your fears to justify, refute, or enable what must occur to overcome that fear, and then based on the knowledge you have about the facts, employ them to realize your fantasies. It is a three-step process, which takes understanding a transition from the unconscious through the preconscious and into the conscious, for you as a leader to be effective in attaining your leadership goals and objectives. This cognitive transition period is where the science and art of coaching becomes most valuable and impactful.

Unfortunately, some leaders who are unable to come to terms with their inherent fears stay in a state of denial and deception, convincing themselves that their state is natural or normal. Yet their inability to relate to others and accomplish seemingly benign tasks remains an issue of concern. Making sound decisions becomes a leadership flaw for such leaders. The transition to leadership effectiveness will be stifled until the leader can identify the fear in his or her subconscious, isolate it, and overcome it with any related facts cultivated in the preconscious mind. The connected cognitive transition to effective employment of strategies that attain one's fantasies sometimes takes external intervention. By external, I mean someone else who understands the processes of the psyche and welcomes rationalization of behaviors and occurrences. This intervention is critical to revealing one's blind spots, unconscious biases, belief systems, or unchallenged perspectives. Research from the Institute of Coaching suggested that about 70 percent of leaders in a study enhanced their effectiveness in relationships, communication with others, and productivity due to the influence of someone else's intervention (leadership coaching)[33]. However, transitioning from a mental state where, as a leader, you feel in control and aware of your challenges or shortcomings to allowing someone to guide you through can be daunting for some, if not for most. Yet it is imperative to push past the nuances that inhibit leadership progress or success so that the leader can effectively employ his or her intellectual capacity to accomplish any desired objectives. The leader will not be able to do so well if the mind is laden with encumbrances, reservations of all kinds, deprivation of intellectual enhancement, or worse, a challenged state of mental health due to past hurts, habits, or repressed developmental, emotional, and psychological trauma. When these cognitive inhibitions are unearthed using the cognitive transition process, it enables the leader to become more effective. Therefore, the model below allows the leadership coach to access and unearth repressed cognitive inhibitions deep in the psyche. These inhibitions in the subconscious mind show up in unconscious behaviors. The cognitive process enables an alignment between an understanding of the mental state and the specific methods to resolve (coach) through the dissonance expressed by employing behavior-modification efforts over time.

---

[33]   Carley Sime, "How Does Coaching Actually Help Leaders?" Forbes, March 28, 2019, retrieved from *https://www.forbes.com/sites/carleysime/2019/03/28/how-does-coaching-actually-help-leaders/?sh=7a66f4df1645.*

THE CONNECTED COGNITIVE PROCESS

To access the subconscious mind of a leader, the leadership health and wellness coach should start by understanding the holistic background of the person. The coach must find out what that person's leadership state is. Is it healthy because the leader is mentally, physically, and emotionally healthy? If the leader is, it is likely that the leader and the organization are well. Understanding one's intellectual, professional, and quite importantly, social background is critical in that initial assessment. Understanding the person's background while undergoing the coaching process is like working from a clear and clean painting canvas or board as an artist. Simple, pointed, and clearly defined questions elicit direct and hopefully undistorted responses, which piece together several likely fragmented and disjointed pieces of information that may be potential clues and insights into the depths of the leader's mind. These will paint an accurate picture of his or her leadership health. You may paint each clue or insight as brush strokes to get a clear picture of where the leader stands in his or her leadership endeavors concerning any details that might have been disclosed. The most practical and realistic methodology to unearth deeply rooted subconscious matters is to be conversational and tactful in questioning. When you think of the mind as having three different sectors (sectors one through three), which you think through to manifest behavior, your questioning process must consider which cognitive sector the leader may be in at a given time so that you can be intentionally impactful.

To access each of these sectors, pointed and directed questioning must be discretely and respectfully asked to help the leader not feel interrogated or intellectually undermined. Instead, you must remain an ally in a problem-resolution or problem-discovery process. To be a partner in the self-discovery process, the leadership health and wellness coach must not at any time create a sense of being the expert at what the client is going through. The client remains the expert. The coach is only there to facilitate, work with, but not direct or diagnose a course of action or ailment. Be informal and conversant with the leader's persona. Don't be rigid, interrogative, or inquisitive but be curious. Allow the leader being coached to volunteer information or readily proclaim his or her state without asking that person to do so. You will certainly not obtain too much information from one session. Therefore, you should schedule a routine, mutually agreed-upon rhythm for conversation. This schedule of meetings or sessions should be marketed or presented as discovery sessions to arrive at specified objectives for each session.

The methodology is simple and deliberate. Start each session using the GOALS method to access each sector of the mind when the time comes. GOALS stands for

G: Goal or the desired outcome for that specific session
O: Objective or the desired milestones to attain that goal
A: Actions or the specific actionable steps to meet the desired objective
L: Limitations or a time period, process, and physical limitations that may potentially need to be overcome to accomplish the actions that meet the objectives for the goal.
S: Support system, the specific desired assistance, tools, or systems to attain the goal within the established timeline

It may take several sessions to uncover as much as feasible from sector one, or it may only take one session. However, as the coach, you should not move on to access sector two without knowing and feeling confident that much information has been gleaned from sector one. The same approach should be employed in sector two before moving to sector three. Ultimately, your focused objective is to work through the leader's challenges to get that person through to sector three where that individual comes to his or her own conclusive realization of courses of action to accomplish and attain desired goals.

During the employment of the GOALS methodology in sector one, you should ask *what* questions as much as feasible until you have exhausted the depth of the desired information. For instance, using our fear of darkness example, the goal (G) for a specific session is to find a way to attend a corporate dinner event at 7:30 p.m. on the following week by first understanding and resolving that a dinner is preferred over a luncheon. The objective (O) is to accept the preference and determine how to get there. The actions (A)are the steps to be taken to overcome the cognitive block for reason the executive leader cannot make it to the dinner because of the time it's being held. There are inherent limitations (L) and timelines to getting to the dinner and determining how to overcome those issues. The support system (S) required to accept the preference and make it to the dinner involves meeting with key stakeholders, providing options to get to the location without driving, etc., to assist and alleviate the anxiety.

Admittedly, this approach is a process that requires a careful and skillful address so that you won't come off to the one being coached as a know-it-all therapist or an investigator. When you exhaust the what questions for this scenario, you should employ the *how* questions, using facts to access sector two to debunk the potential fears or inherent limitations. The facts will alleviate the real or perceived limitations and allow practical, actionable steps to meet the desired objective. Evidently, the coach being prepared to ask questions such as how one will overcome the limitations or accomplish steps to success is encouraging, and it elicits an air of worthy undertaking instead of a chore. Remember, naturally, as humans, any path one perceives as work, self-limiting, or demotivating will likely be avoided, ignored, or dismissed. The leader must find it rewarding, competitive, and compelling to pursue an effort and realize the goal. When the facts of the objectives toward the goal are exhausted, letting the leader proclaim, decide on, or discover how to accomplish or attain that goal will require placing a sense of compulsion on actions and limitations to meet the goal. You will need to attain this deadline by asking *when* questions. Specifically, ask when the objectives will be met to accomplish the desired goal. Conclusively, he or she needs accountability to meet the goal by walking through the limitations, actions, or objectives. Over time, the goal will certainly help the leader become successful. Leaders become more effective, resilient, and aware of who they are and what it takes to get them to overcome any unconscious behaviors deeply rooted in their subconscious mind. Figure 3 below illustrates the relationship among the sectors.

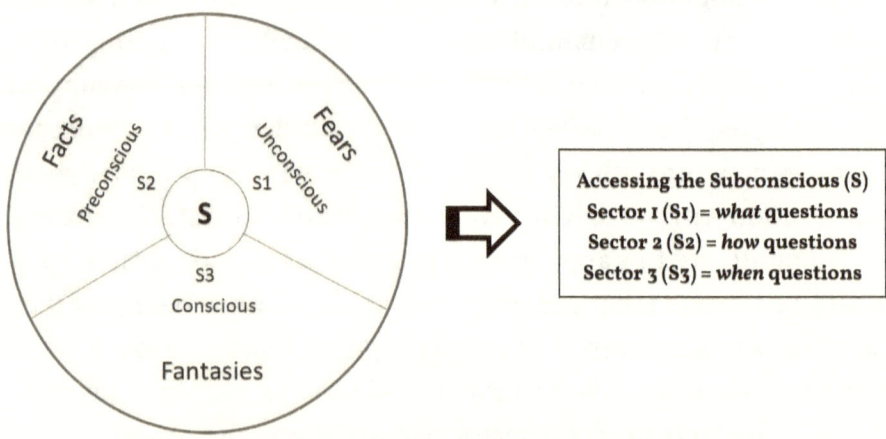

Figure 3. Connected Cognitive Approach to Leadership Health and Wellness Coaching

THE CONNECTED COGNITIVE PROCESS EXEMPLIFIED

To explain the cognitive process in the given example of this text, let's suppose this is the first session with the executive leader who desires to uncover what holds him or her back from being mission effective in accomplishing desired goals or in the context of this scenario, not enthusiastic and dreading going to this corporate dinner event. You should begin to understand the professional, intellectual, and social background to enable you as the coach to build credibility with the leader. You will be able to do so while piecing together potential clues for why things appear the way they potentially do. Paint the picture of the leader's mind as free-form conversation ensues. With GOALS in mind, your hypothetical session may go something like this:

Leader: "Thank you for taking the time to chat with me today. So, what exactly are we going to do? What do you want to know, and how long is this going to take?" Pick up on diction and tone that suggest a sense of anxiety, discomfort, absence of information, and curiosity, which must be eased by the coach.

Coach: "It's my pleasure! Well, thanks for asking all those important questions. My sole goal as your coach is to work with you to understand how we can continue to develop excellent strategies of efficiencies and impact in your organization by understanding your broad, remarkable accomplishments, which have earned you the role or position you're in today. Please share what led you to create such an impact in your career." Acknowledge personal or professional excellence, achievement, and impact by showing interest in the leader's background.

Leader: "Well, I started my career as an accounts manager ..." Allow the conversation to unfold by talking less and interjecting briefly, when feasible, to ask direct open-ended questions, which start with what like, "What is your family background?" or "What is unique or what are you amost proud of about your background?" These should engender a wealth of clues and coaching points.

Coach: "What desired outcome would you like to see from our session today?" (goal) This question is very broad and might yield unrealistic goals, desires, or expectations from the client. However, though it may not be attained within the given session period, it gives you more insight into an ultimate or future desired goal and outcome. Make sure to ask the desired expectation when narrowed to an achievable goal and outcome for the session.

Leader: "I need to figure out why making people understand the strategic implications of taking time away from personal time is so hard. Why am I the only one who's convinced there should be a luncheon instead of a dinner so that I can present the corporate awards? Everyone else thinks the corporate event should be a candlelight dinner instead of a luncheon. I don't think so at all. In fact, I absolutely advise against it. Help me understand if I am off the mark here in my thoughts." A key indicator that there is a leadership systemic problem with a cognitive challenge is how vehemently opposed to a course of action one can get or can be to an idea that is almost insignificant or irrelevant. Tone, diction, and perspectives are insightful if you tune in to hear the arguments. In this context, it doesn't matter whether the event is a luncheon or dinner, although the preference is a dinner in this case because of the desired atmosphere for an award ceremony. However, the key words or phrases from the leader that indicate anxiety, fear, or reservation are "I," "absolutely," "why am I the only one," and "everyone else thinks." A classic case of I versus them or everyone else is wrong, and I am right can spell a coaching concern. These are the indicators of how well the leader is to create a healthy environment.

Coach: "I mean, what can we accomplish in today's session? So what makes you think you are off the mark in your thought, and what makes everyone else prefer dinner over a luncheon?" (refined goal question and objective). While accessing sector one (S1), using the leader's own words on thoughts to get into another layer of depth compels the leader to think or reconsider the legitimacy and relevance of his or her own perspective if the leader lacks self-awareness yet seeks to be introspective.

Leader: "Well, I don't know, and I don't think I am off the mark. I just think a luncheon is better because we can all drive there straight from work, we don't have to take any time off after work, everyone is already here for us to carpool, and I think I make a pretty good case for holding it at lunch instead of dinner." Clearly, the coach should pick up on the egocentrism in the diction of "I just think" and little about what others think or propose. Secondly, the diction of "we can all drive" and "already here for us to carpool" seemingly justify why the luncheon is a better preference, as it serves the ego's purpose. Additionally, it avoids the inherent fear of darkness and therefore, driving in it, which lies at the crux of the preference.

Coach: "What will you do to convince everyone else that the luncheon is better than a dinner and that you absolutely advise against it?" (actions) This approach and line of inquiry quickly leads the leader to realize that he or she now has the burden of creating value and significance contrary to the populace, convention, or established norms. This approach may be a point of introspection and reflection to make a case for the contrary. At this point, when the leader realizes they have no facts or compelling depth to his or her position, the coach can transition to sector two and ask the how questions. This line of inquiry stimulates thoughts for options and possibilities to arrive at a resolution for the ultimate desired outcome or goal.

Leader: "I don't know. I think I will explain the benefits of using working hours during the day versus evening, and it costs less for a luncheon than a dinner." Arguments for the leader's position, though seemingly legitimate, may appear to all revolve around every excuse not to hold the event at night while ignoring the value it brings and everyone else's preference. The working-hours argument is unfounded because it results in lost productivity or cost of man-hours. In this case, the leader is lucidly oblivious to his or her excuses and drives attention toward self and not an others' consensus.

Coach: "How will you explain that your preference has more value in enhancing the company climate and spirit than what every committee member's vote prefers" (still actions). The shift to sector two (S2) now requires using facts to debunk or overcome the fear. The line of inquiry now compels a more thought-provoking approach to the method of employment to justify or make sense of the belief. This cognitive probe for a legitimate and cogent response may spark a moment of self-awareness.

Leader: "Well, I will show them the cost savings in terms of luncheon versus dinner and how research proves that employees need more time off away from work to enhance their quality of life and performance at work." Notice that the desired effort to show the cost savings and researched quality of life information still defies the fact that the committee has voted unanimously on a preference. Additionally, it doesn't consider the enhanced morale booster for improving the company climate, which the staff looks forward to. Until this point, every effort suggests an agenda that discards evidence or defies logic, which in this case, has been the consensus of the committee.

Coach: "How will the committee and staff feel about the company's leadership when they realize their votes don't count and their preference for a dinner has been trumped by cost savings and quality of life research?" (limitations) This question further delves into the leader's judgment to solicit his or her introspection. This second layer of *how* questions should compel a heightened awareness, which reveals the depth of the flawed perspective.

Leader: "Well, that will not be good, will it? It will decrease morale and affect the company climate and spirit. I guess I should accept their preference, shouldn't I?"

Coach: "When will you accept their preference and let them know that it's OK to have a dinner versus a luncheon?" (limitation) The shift to sector three (S3) confines and compels a defined time to accomplish the desired outcome. In this case, it will confirm that his or her perception was flawed and that the leader needed to understand why the dinner was a preferred option.

Leader: "I need to figure out how I can make the team aware of my support of the award ceremony and dinner. I just need to ensure everyone understands me."

Coach: "When will you get the team together to explain your thoughts and sentiments so that we can arrange what it will take to get there" (support system). This question compels a timeline for establishing a support system and strategy to accomplish the goal. Notice that the overall problem has not been resolved in this session. The underlying problem of fear of darkness still exists, and it will ultimately be addressed to overcome the leader's cognitive dissonance or reservation with this particular situation.

As a health and wellness coach for leaders, you are a change agent—positioned to bring resolve to an otherwise troubled and encumbered leader, who desires transformation but doesn't know how. In a few cases, the leader knows he or she needs help, but the leader cannot muster the courage to do so. This is where your intuition, approach, and mastery of self and substance come in. Your sole focus and objective are to reveal the leader's inherent strengths and capacity over their BS with clarity of purpose and mind. This revelation can only occur effectively when you know yourself and how to relate to those who may not know themselves as well. After all, you are a coach. You have to be a leader in your own right to lead another leader through a stepped path of self-discovery. Therefore, understanding how S1 through S3 brings relief, resolve, and revelation of truths to a leader is ultimately a result of your mastery of the skill and art of leadership health and wellness coaching.

CHAPTER 9

How to Use the Seven-Layer-Deep Questioning Technique to Achieve Leadership Success

The noblest question in the world is:
"What good may I do in it?"

—Benjamin Franklin
(Founding father of the United States)

QUESTIONING IN COACHING is primarily an art and skill developed over time to elicit the desired behavioral responses and to trigger self-awareness notions, which enable action. For leaders, questioning must be very intentional, strategic, and conversational. An inquisitive, directive, or interrogative approach will not work. It is self-limiting, self-defeating, and almost always a career killer because nearly all leaders, business or otherwise, have egos that must be acknowledged. We all have them. The ego is a natural psychological attribute, which sets us apart from others and makes us successful in life if we express it properly. How we carry it or demonstrate it is another story. Without ego, we will be limited in our drive to succeed. Therefore, questioning a leader about how well he or she is performing and how he or she needs to perform is an attempt to question the effectiveness of the ego in attaining results. The seven-layers-deep questioning technique is one that I have adopted to elicit underlying truths or the root cause of one's actions. The origin of this reasoning method is unclear but useful in understanding why one does or desires something. Using the technique, I have developed and applied the same technique to connect with leaders without being intrusive and absurd in my questions. I play on the words *ice* and *ear* for the acronym ICCEEAR to suggest that anything that is on ice is cool and calm, as in the expression "placing someone on ice" to mean you've kept that person cool. Lending an ear to someone who needs it is at the core of what a leadership health and wellness coach who engages in active listening should be about. I have named each layer of questioning to provide the coach with a rationale for why that question is essential to the leader.

The layers of questioning are open-ended and conversational, using the word *what*. This first set of questions intends to build rapport and earn your client's trust after the first session, which was likely focused on getting all the administrative protocols out of the way. In any event, those moments are also critical in building rapport and trust with the client. The seven-layers-deep questions are in the following context:

Layer 1. Icebreaker: "What was the highlight of your day or week?"
Layer 2. Connection: "What brings you joy most about [X]?"
Layer 3. Control: "What aspect of [X] can you control?"

Layer 4. **E**ngagement: "What about [X] empowers you to lead?"

Layer 5. **E**mpowerment: "What should [X] look like when completed?"

Layer 6. **A**chievement: "What should [X] feel like and do for you when complete?'

Layer 7. **R**esolution: "What do you feel without [X]?"

By layer seven, you have determined what this leader specifically misses about X that will continue to bring the leader joy if controlled, attained, and evident. Responses to these questions are context clues shaping what is most important to the leader. Notice that the result is what the leader considers the day's highlight, but the ultimate reason it was a highlight was because of how or what it would have made the leader feel without it. The only reason to end this sequence of questioning on a negative note ("feel without it") instead of always on a positive note is to remind both the leader and the coach what to work on or what the leader does not want to feel. It is to uncover or discover a core or sore area of focus to coach through if there is ever an absence. It is to put back into the leader's life whatever the X is.

Consequently, this will engender a goal to work on for resolution. Humans are emotional beings, and they rarely, if ever, take action on logic. We take action on emotion and justify it with logic. This is the ultimate selling principle that marketers and exceptional salespeople have known and have explored for years. The same principle applies to helping a leader come to his or her own measure of self-awareness to attain the leader's desired goals and objectives, no matter how austere they may appear.

REASONING SEVEN LAYERS DEEP

To appreciate the value of this technique and its implications to the coach and the leader, you should understand the value desired by the leader. What does the leader really want to accomplish? What is the leader willing to forgo or overcome to attain the desire? Understanding the reasoning behind the leader's desired result may come from a wellness vision or the ICCEEAR approach. When you can obtain the desired effect or feeling from the leader, you can help the leader develop the strategic actions and goals that attain the expected, deep-rooted result. Consequently, as the coach, you discover the reasoning behind what the leader wants without asking, "Why?" This is critical to developing a plan with the leader on how to attain his or her desired results.

I once had a coaching session with a business leader who was intrigued by how my business structure, systems, and processes were set up. During the session, instead of answering the questions I asked, he shifted the focus toward me and started asking me questions about how I accomplished the things I did. In that case, as the coach, you clearly have to set the boundaries of who is asking questions and who should be answering them without creating a sense of resentment or discomfort. Notice that this leader was curious, and instead of keeping the focus on what the session was about, he was more interested in my success at what I was doing than his own. A client like that can throw you off your game or process and can make it a little difficult for you to really understand the reasoning behind his willingness to be coached in the first place. Is it to understand how to get better holistically, or is it that he is just curious about the entire coaching process? Therefore, adopting this questioning method to get to the heart of why one really does what one does sheds significant light on how you approach the coaching relationship.

EMPLOYING ACTIVE LISTENING TO REASONING

When a leader does not want to discuss a topic that may be seemingly uncomfortable or hard to assimilate, working with the leader to arrive at a heightened state of self-awareness that compels action is imperative. Three approaches are essential to understand why the leader considers one course of action over another.

1. Listen without saying a word except "tell me more."
2. Listen and reflect back to the leader their statements
3. Listen and say nothing back to the leader.

The third option is the least preferred. To understand what the leader feels and desires to do using this approach may require you to transition earlier or quicker from *what* series of questions to the *how* questions, when it is evident that the leader has decided that he or she knows what is needed to accomplish and realize his or her resolve. For instance, the following statements may be an attempt to get to their methodology and to arrive at their desired course of action:

- How are you enjoying your progress so far?
- How well do you think you get your team, or your team gets you?
- How much control do you feel about this situation on a scale of one to ten?
- How will you take action on your decision to modify your leadership approach? (*Don't* say change your behavior.)
- How will you know that you are content with the course of action you are about to take?
- How important is modifying your approach to your leadership success?
- How will not accomplishing this behavior change make you feel about your progress?

Responses to these questions may be brief but very informative on the core reason why the leader behaves or is in his or her state. Remember that these open-ended questions are not to be asked directly with *how* as the first word because it may seem like an interrogation. However, it is intended to be conversational. These are leaders who have a sense of pride and accomplishment and who are trying to solicit your skills to help them through a rough spot, so make it conversational. I would consider the first icebreaker layer of question to look something like this:

> "Don, it appears you have clearly identified what you enjoy most about leading your great team of professionals, and I am curious to know how you are enjoying your progress so far since we've been working together?" After the response, you then get to the next one. "Really! Great to hear! Interesting. You know, I wonder how well you think your team gets you if you have obviously been doing quite well."

The dialogue should smoothly transition from one line of questioning to another without a sense of feeling interrogated or barraged with questions. As you can see, the question is embedded in a conversation but is clearly open-ended enough not to get lost in transmission and translation.

One of the most critical aspects in the coaching relationship is the step one takes toward action to attain the desired results. Action for change and action to address outstanding or pending gaps takes employing the most important and open-ended question in the dialogue: "When?" Therefore, a line of inquiry might sound something like this:

> "I am glad that you have clearly identified the steps you need to take to address some of the essential aspects of your organization's goals and ensure that you are well-positioned to succeed. So when do you

think you will be able to start taking steps toward your immediate goals?"

The first part of what you say is to set the stage or foundation for the question you are about to ask so that it doesn't appear to be or create the sense of being interrogative. Therefore, you acknowledge the efforts of achievement and desired actions the person has taken or is poised to take. This allows the question to be received well as a step toward achieving desired goals.

Every leadership health and wellness coach must practice active listening skills to become adept at their value because responses to those questions reveal the most important critical insights to bridging any gaps in the leader's livelihood. When, as the coach, you can understand the reasoning behind why someone takes a course of action over another and can piece together any broken aspects of the leader's life, you bring relief. You have taken time to resolve a situation that would otherwise be left unaddressed. Otherwise, dreams are shattered, and more often than not, a leader is left with a life laden with a whole lot of baggage he or she may carry into the workplace. This kind of pain may ultimately cause undue displeasure to those around them.

ACHIEVING SUCCESS WITH ICCEEAR

I am often asked what success is. I have always given the same response: Success is being able to attain what one sets out to do while realizing what one considers to be a worthy ideal. Success is different for everyone. It is measured only by the one who sets the bar to measure the success of that ideal. In helping a leader overcome unhealthy decision-making or lifestyle choices, which impacts his or her ability to lead effectively, the coach must be passionately sensitive to the leader's needs to succeed. Success takes working closely and meticulously with the leader so that you can arrive at a plan where a wellness goal and healthy action path is set for the leader to execute. If there is a need to solicit external, expert help by other specialists, that should be clearly articulated by the coach to the leader on the boundaries of their scope of practice. When you look up the word success, you have a number of definitions from varied sources, including the *Merriam-Webster's Dictionary*, the *Cambridge Dictionary,* and *dictionary.com*. One of the definitions from *dictionary.com* puts it plainly: "the favorable or prosperous termination of attempts or endeavors; the accomplishment of one's goals." This definition is what leadership coaching should aim to accomplish—helping others properly terminate unfruitful and unhealthy attempts or endeavors to lead well. When a leader can successfully lead his or her team toward a clearly defined path on a journey, which indicates clearly defined goals, the whole team members' outcomes are rewarding, and they can be replicated for better results. Success, therefore, means different things to different people and at different stages of their lives. What I would like to see in the life of someone who comes to me for support differs from what that person would like to see for his or her own life. To achieve success, it is incumbent on the coach to effectively communicate the scope of service and performance to the client and to have the client define his or her measure of success at a given space of time. The coaching client must define success.

I had the privilege of coaching a retired corporate executive in his late sixties. He had been a hardworking leader, who was committed to building systems and processes that affected the company's overall health. He had retired from a very wealthy corporate job six years earlier, he was now working on his health and also on his social relationships, so I was glad to take him on. One thing that was quite evident with this client from the outset was that he loved the prestige and aura of being responsible for a very prominent nonprofit organization, which kept him extremely busy. He was so busy that he could hardly schedule his own personal life to shape the course or direction of his health. As a leadership health and wellness coach, what I found intriguing for this ideal client was isolating his love for solving world hunger from his need to fix his health. He was stressed and was distressed inside. He did all but refused to acknowledge the two had to know their places, otherwise, nothing would be successfully achieved. He was late for appointments. He would not eat or attempt to align his schedule with his personal health. Ultimately, we terminated the coaching relationship. The point is that unless one knows what one wants and is committed to getting after it, you, as the coach, have a steep hill to climb with that person if he or she is to succeed.

Let's use ICCEEAR to reach an ambivalent and unfocused client by assessing the seven basic success approaches that probe cognitive action.

Interest: Determine or develop interest or inspiration for mental health and wellness.

Conditions: Determine whether current conditions provide the right time for change.

Capacity: Assess whether the client has the capacity (lifestyle) to endure the change process.

Environment: Encourage a conducive environment that facilitates enhanced change.

Examples: Provide referenced examples of successful outcomes and work toward them.

Actions: Support and facilitate bold actions toward health and wellness mindset changes.

Reward: Provide positive reinforcement for small victories. Celebrate them!

When leaders feel bombarded by multiple decision-making challenges at every turn of the day, they must have clarity on what decisions demand the most attention when it requires practice. Sometimes, it requires having a seasoned leadership health and wellness coach in their corners too. So considering the success approach highlighted above, put into perspective and consider a client who is troubled or disturbed by all the things he or she has to accomplish quickly to keep that client's sanity. After establishing your initial rapport and groove with that individual, you are obligated to find out what makes him or her happiest or what is most impactful. You have ICCEEAR in mind as you engage in dialogue. Remember, leaders do not like being interrogated. They always like to exercise and exhibit control and comfort. So you determine what inspires them. Is this leader currently at a place where the conditions are ripe to start taking small steps toward the desired change in his or her life—whatever that change might be? Often, a self-limiting belief or bleak course of action will bring relief to his or her cause. Understanding what kind of schedule the client runs, will he or she have the capacity to take on little changes that would help alleviate problems? If so, you should encourage that person to set the right environment to achieve the desired effort. Give examples of what success looks like, and when it is evident that your client feels a sense of compulsion to take action and move toward changes, be supportive. Be informative and forthcoming with overwhelming support. Provide feedback and more importantly, celebrate any victories that you make together.

CHAPTER 10

How to Map Leadership Goals to Leadership Health and Wellness

A leader is one who knows the way, goes the way,
and shows the way.

—John C. Maxwell
(Leadership expert and author)

As a leader, one of the most important things needed to make an impact in any sphere of influence is the establishment of strategic and operational goals that a leader with a team wants to accomplish. Therefore, it's important to identify organizational goals and to align team leadership health and wellness efforts for them. Otherwise, a broken, depressed, discouraged, and overworked team can never effectively attain the organizational goals. All it takes is one troubled team member, often referred to as the weakest link, to draw the vitality, reputation, and credibility of your organization's objectives down. To that end, identifying a clearly defined set of organizational goals and a stepped process of mapping healthy practices and wellness initiatives to those goals cannot be taken for granted. The outline below suggests a notional leadership goals strategy mapped to a health and wellness process to achieve operational success.

Understanding how the three pillars of leadership health and wellness (physical, social, and mental) interplay in goal mapping requires a strategically planned approach at each level of the wellness continuum. This means that at level one, as the organizational leader, you must have a goal to be self-aware of where your leadership tank is. Are you running on empty with your health by staying stressed or ill-rested? Are you creating an environment that is not well or conducive to effective operational leadership in the workplace? For instance (physically), because you are not getting enough sleep, you walk into work looking like a zombie. Maybe you are so physically out of shape that you can barely keep up with meetings without losing your breath. I remember watching a 20/20 excerpt where the late Barbara Walters was interviewing a prominent political figure. In one of the questions, she literally acknowledged that she wasn't sure how to ask the question but figured she would anyway. She blatantly stated and asked him about the effect of being significantly overweight! After he acknowledged that he was, she asked, "Why?" Imagine what that question does to one's ego (mental), subordinates (social), and feelings (physical state). Can you imagine a question like that on national TV—a leader admitting that he was not in the best physical shape as he ought to be? My guess is that besides the likely palm sweats and feelings of heat, which he may have experienced in the moment around the collar of his shirt as he sat there in his suit, it compelled a series of follow-on actions for him on how he related to his team from that point forward. So think about what that means to your team for a moment—a negative image of what you look like and represent to the organization and its people. Worse yet, what if you have a hostile working relationship with some, if not most, in the organization? As if that weren't bad enough, you probably could not adequately focus on a topic and discuss it through a meeting without losing your train of thought or showing a lapse in judgment. The combined effects of these three aspects, physical, social, and mental flaws in any leader do not work well for enhancing credibility and sound judgment for his or her team. Consequently, understanding the relationship between your goal level and the pillar of leadership health and wellness that they map should help shape your actions and objectives toward success as depicted in Figure 4 below.

Strategic Mapping Level	Goal Attainment (Leadership Quality)	Leadership Health and Wellness Objective (Leadership Health and Wellness Pillar)
One	Self-awareness (introspection)	Define who you are to your organization (physical, social, and mental).
Two	Self-direction (integrity)	Determine when you will establish a process to attain specified goals (mental).
Three	Self-confidence (assertiveness)	Decide and express how you will maintain your influence to accomplish your daily mission (mental and social).
Four	Self-growth (discipline)	Decide how you will establish a growth mindset with your professional team (mental).
Five	Self-assessment (competitiveness)	Annotate how you will measure professional performance and success (physical, social, and mental).

Figure 4. Mapping Leadership Goal Level
to Health and Wellness Objective

MAPPING GOAL LEVEL TO LEADERSHIP HEALTH AND WELLNESS PILLARS

Goal 1: Mapping Self-Awareness (Introspection) to Define Who You Are to Your Organization

An introspective leader will align all efforts and concerns with any feedback that his or her organization provides, to enhance leadership impact and performance. Mapping self-awareness to organizational transparency implies that the leader solicits, welcomes, and projects team members' perspectives to help shape the organization's goals. The team knows and understands the leader, and you, as the leader, know where you stand with them. There is no guessing. There is no ambiguity or surprises when it comes to communicating and fostering the organization's path forward because the team has been involved in the leadership process from the outset. All goals ought to build upon this first level of goal setting. Without this fundamental level, the risk of retention increases due to team members not feeling a part of forging the organization's future. The potential for the disconnection between leadership decision-making and reality increases significantly, and few feel they belong. A self-aware leader understands the value of any impact that he or she creates and ways to ensure that decisive action and objectives are for the greater good. When this first level is well-grounded and transparency exists between you and those you lead, reflecting on how you can improve behavior or conduct is not a chore or an uncomfortable endeavor. Instead, it is healthier and soothing, as it takes away any measure of undue stress and compulsion to please anyone in particular. To be introspective, all three pillars are expressed.

Physical

The physical pillar allows you to examine how you carry yourself and remain conscious of the example of physical health you exemplify. An unhealthy leader undermines the measure of influence and credibility required to lead because no one will take the leader seriously if that leader appears careless in his or her physical appearance. A physically healthy leader is just as self-conscious of staying in good physical shape and health as one who seems out of shape, unkempt, or limited by physical stamina to lead and perform at his or her peak. The only distinguishing factor between the two is that the former took action and overcame any mental inhibitions that precluded achieving his or her desired goals. Being self-aware matters. But being driven and disciplined to achieve wellness matters more.

Social

A self-aware leader who socially engages the team and solicits performance feedback by including team members in the organizational policy and development process will succeed. This leadership approach compels the leader to consciously and effectively engage with team members from a position of comfort and approachability, without feeling overly self-conscious, misjudged, or distant due to how the team relates to the leader.

Mental

A clear conscience and state of mind for a self-aware leader does not mean guessing what everyone on the team thinks, nor does it mean consistently asking team members to submit suggestions for organizational improvements. A culture of inclusion and participative leadership will enhance opportunities for self-improvement.

The leader who incorporates a culture of transparency and clarity of purpose into the team's operational processes is likely the least stressed and aloof to the organization's well-being. Goal 1, therefore, prepares the leader to excel by establishing the basis for building wellness in self-awareness. Without coming to terms with this level of self-awareness, it will be challenging to move onto and set the goals for the second level, when one must become assertive and self-confident to influence others.

Goal 2: Mapping Self-Direction (Integrity) to Determine When You Will Establish a Process to Attain Specified Goals

Self-direction stems from the need to have and exercise integrity in all you do. This leads to the establishment of processes to attain any desired goals that you may have if you are to stay viable as a leader. I would argue that integrity is the bedrock of any system you implement if you want to achieve your goals. For instance, if a real estate agent lacks the integrity to maintain ethical standards while conducting client operations, the processes that individual implements, such as fiscal transactions with partners or legal firms, will quickly disintegrate. This will occur because his or her character flaw now impacts others, including your client. Therefore, effectively applying this leadership quality of integrity to every aspect of your professional well-being (systems and processes) opens the doors of success widely to realize your goals. I consider a leader's health at this goal level even more fundamental than the previous goal because without integrity, your actions, credibility, and success as a leader is void. Being self-directed or driven is a mental obligation you must overcome to excel. For you to exercise sound leadership health, linking integrity to a clearly defined process for goal attainment ultimately establishes your credibility and fosters your objectivity to take the right actions on time.

Goal 3: Mapping Self-Confidence (Assertiveness) to Decide and Express the Way You Will Maintain Your Influence to Accomplish Your Daily Mission

Goal-level 3 builds on level 2 by recognizing the value of assertiveness in maintaining influence among team members to accomplish desired organizational objectives. When leaders prepare well to excel, confidence in what they do is self-evident. At this level, a leader cannot take the objective of executing daily operations lightly if they are to attain goals.

Mental

If you lack the drive, autonomy, confidence, or influence to empower the people around you to achieve professional objectives, you'll likely be unhealthy in this aspect of your leadership. Therefore, identifying what makes you confidently effective as a leader is paramount to what makes you professionally successful in leading a team to success. Sometimes it may take practicing your daily routine in front of a mirror to feel confident in your decisive actions.

Social

Sometimes, it may take starting with a small group of leaders or team members you trust to discuss and obtain insights or recommendations on your approach. Often, it will take boldness to stand in front of or with your entire team and to do it afraid and nervous. The more you do it, the more assertive and confident you will get. This consistency will make you healthy, not only mentally but also socially, as you build credibility to the next level.

Goal 4: Mapping Self-Growth (Discipline) to Decide the Way You Will Establish a Growth Mindset with Your Professional Team

Admittedly, this is likely the most challenging level to attain, which most leaders don't particularly do well in. Their leadership wellness in self-growth, due to a disciplined lifestyle, is lacking. Evidently, the mental mindset to identify what cultural or lifestyle choices inhibit a consistent and focused lifestyle to develop as a leader is important. Truthfully, you cannot give what you do not have as a leader if you cannot discipline yourself well enough to have a self-growth routine. This means having an insatiable quest for knowledge through reading, training, research, self-improvement initiatives, or anything that compels you to consciously and consistently add value to yourself so that you can add value to others. I have struggled with this aspect of leadership at different stages in my leadership journey. Yet now, I understand that having a calendar that schedules everything I do and an alarm that reminds me to do them can only work effectively if I commit to acknowledging them. If it's time to take a break to read a book for half an hour at a specific time every day, schedule and execute it. It is the one sure way to attain leadership wellness with your team. Your team is only as good as the place you lead them and how much you pour into them. Be well so that your professional team can also stay well.

Goal 5: Mapping Self-Assessment (Competitiveness) to Annotate the Way You Will Measure Professional Performance and Success

You have to measure what you expect. You have to know where you stand in your world and industry. You have to track your progress to know whether you are hitting your targets. You have to examine yourself almost as often as you examine your financial health to determine whether you are competing in the marketplace or are lagging. Healthy competitiveness as a leadership attribute in any organization means that you are measuring your performance against market demands, which are evident with another entity in the same industry, sector, or marketplace. Your metric for comparison should align with your goals for success. Having a competitive advantage or market-dominating position over others in your industry suggests that you are the obvious choice for what you offer. Jeff Bezos of Amazon or Tim Cook of Apple are the obvious choices for all things merchandise or electronics, respectively. So how will you become the obvious choice for the things you offer to whomever you offer them to, to the extent that you stand out as healthy and well in all aspects of your organization? Let's look at the following.

Mental

Your professional performance depends significantly on your cognitive ability to distinguish between where you are currently and where you desire to be in context and in relation to other competitors in the market. This is why standards, analytical metrics, feasibility studies, market research, and the like are important. They provide you with the level of analytical rigor you need to stay informed and to be competitive. Your success's performance measure starts with having in mind and hopefully annotated a clearly defined, determined, and measurable outcome to reach your goal so that you know when you have attained or surpassed it.

Social

Your social health to be competitive for success depends on how well you are meeting your customer or client needs. Competitive leaders employ customer or client feedback mechanisms, such as surveys, questionnaires, or other data collection means, to assess the health of their organization. If you are not socially healthy to stay competitive, you risk not being viable. Consequently, using "tell us how we are doing" as a cultural practice across your social platform systems to gauge your health is essential.

Physical

Nothing beats being physically present and aware of your current state if you want to take an active role in being competitively successful. When you want to excel in anything, you cannot be passive or indifferent in your approach to drive the desired results. An Olympian doesn't show up for practice once a week, or a professional footballer doesn't practice his or her plays casually. A successful restaurateur doesn't stay at home and hire a manager to run the restaurant without checking in often or always being there to offer the highest caliber of service to patrons. Therefore, to be professionally successful, you have to be physically engaged. Overall, successful leaders adequately demonstrate a healthy balance of physical, social, and mental approaches to the way they self-assess to reassess their successes.

When the leadership health and wellness coach maps these aspects of a leader's wellness with leadership goals, it enables the leader client to have a more precise road map or way forward. That leader understands how every course of action taken can either significantly impact or diminish the credibility and performance of the leader and consequently, the health of his or her organization. Therefore, understanding the connection between health and attaining professional goals is imperative and indisputably essential.

CHAPTER 11

How to Bridge the Leadership Gap between the Unconscious Mind and Behavior

Although we cannot intentionally change many aspects of ourselves or our world, we can exert some power over the courses of our own lives.

—James O. Prochaska
(Canadian American psychologist)

THERE IS A significant gap between what leaders think they know about themselves and what they actually do, especially when they are not self-aware. Most leaders acquire a set of belief systems to shape their mindset and behaviors by the time they reach higher leadership positions. These beliefs sometimes become systemic and engrained into their organizational culture while others are specifically inherent with the leaders, depending on how influential they are. When a leader has a gap in knowledge, skill, or ability, this gap often accompanies a glaring lapse in judgment or decision-making. It is because the leader doesn't know. An American saying goes, "When you know better, you do better!" I am unsure if this is the case for leaders who know they don't know but refuse to delegate their areas of weakness. To overcome or bridge this leadership gap, you must understand your client and the unconscious impulses that compel his or her behaviors. To this end, the need for a change stimulus (corrective action) becomes invaluable for execution. I recommend five strategies to help bridge the leadership gap in the quest to be healthy and an organizational leader. Where there are gaps in knowledge, skills, abilities, judgment, and decision-making, apply the coaching bridges or change the stimuli of educate, demonstrate, collaborate, deliberate, and participate, respectively. Since the unconscious mind tends to respond spontaneously to external stimuli when prompted or provoked, without the right cognitive filter, you will likely obtain an undesirable response. Understanding how the change-stimuli influence the leader's actions and decision-making is imperative to know how to approach the coaching relationship with the client. Figure 5 illustrates the coaching approach to bridge the leadership gap that leads to undesirable behavior.

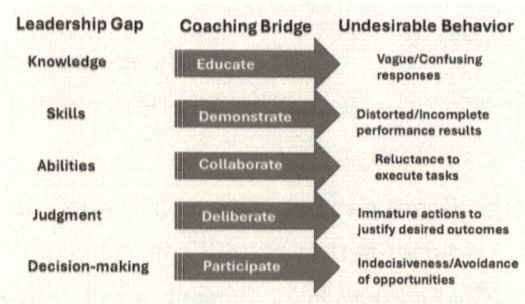

Figure 5. Leadership Gap Coaching Bridge

To bridge the gap between the unconscious mind and behavior, you must first recognize a gap in cognitive performance as illustrated in the graphic above. To mask a knowledge gap, a leader may be unaware of the unconscious behavior he or she elicits, such as providing vague, long, and confusing responses to simple questions asked. To highlight this phenomenon, I like the example of asking the blind man to describe what an elephant looks like. Instead of admitting that he or she doesn't know due to blindness, the leader begins to describe it based on the prior touch and feel of the animal's trunks, preconceived as the state of the whole. So as far as this person knows, the elephant is long and skinny. The knowledge gap here is not the description of the animal from the leader's perspective, but it is negligence to mention that his or her knowledge is limited by blindness and that the description stems from an initial impression.

Bridging gaps between cognitive states and behavior is not only an imperative but also critical for connecting a leader's strengths with his or her desired outcomes. When you engage a leader in a coaching relationship to address key areas of concern, the method of identifying where there is a disconnect in existent gaps is by soliciting a self-critique or an introspective approach to his or her leadership health and wellness.

LEVERAGING THE CHANGE STIMULUS

To leverage the change stimulus that affects behavior, assessing the fundamental health of the leader takes precedence over any other need. The change stimulus may be introducing a reading regimen to close the knowledge gap. Another change stimulus might be a practical workshop or master class to close the skills gap and a strength's challenge to close the abilities gap. Overall, leveraging the change stimulus early in the coaching relationship means that as the coach, you will identify the leader's strengths to stay connected with that individual's cognitive approach or mindset and behavior. For instance, if the coach realizes that the leader has an aptitude for intellectual enhancement, the need to introduce that leader to a specific type of literature interest will soon maximize or build upon his or her effectiveness and excellence. This occurs by building confidence and character earlier in the coaching relationship to be able to facilitate change in the behavior of the leader.

When leveraging the change stimulus, whether it is a reading regimen or a master class, the phenomenal value of consistency is imperative to reinforce. Stimuli that are employed only once or twice in a projected space of time are usually ineffective. To modify behavior, repetition matters. Employing the change stimuli in the leader's coaching process to positively connect the unconscious mind to behavior will ultimately enhance the efficacy of the leader's effectiveness. However, to achieve the desired level of effectiveness, attending the master class consistently for its duration and applying its tenets during that period would increase the opportunity for behavior modification. Additionally, providing the leader with a reading regimen attached to an outcome deliverable on a routine schedule also increases the leader's accountability and the sustainability of that behavior.

EMPLOYING THE TRANS THEORETICAL MODEL OF BEHAVIOR CHANGE (TTM) TO TRIPLE C

Triple C enhances a leader's self-awareness by eliciting behavior modification based on the trans theoretical model of behavior change (TTM) or stages of change, which are propounded by psychologist Dr. James Prochaska and Carlo DiClemente.[34] It enables the leadership health and wellness coach to know what stage of readiness for change the client is

---

[34]   James O. Prochaska and John C. Norcross, "Stages of change," *Psychotherapy: Theory, Research, Practice, Training*, 38, no. 4 (2001) 443.

in so that efforts to modify behavior and attain a desired outcome can occur. When a leader undergoes a change process, it is usually over a projected period. Rarely do leaders modify behavior on the fly, especially when they have preprogrammed biases in their subconscious minds over time. Coaching through the abovementioned model is imperative to alter behaviors that manifest the unconscious mind. Since it takes time to change or modify behavior, the leadership health and wellness coach must be patient and appreciative of where the client is on the continuum of the change process. These are the stages in Figure 6:

Stages of Change	Readiness for change	Strategy to Influence Cognitive Change
Pre-contemplation	Not ready	Rehearse reflections on any sustaining talk.
Contemplation	Not ready	State the benefits and reflections of a changed state.
Preparation	Ready	Foster change talk to build confidence.
Action	Ready	Coach to the identified gaps in the action steps.
Maintenance	Sustained	Request periodic updates on impact of sustainment.
Termination	Confirmed	Celebrate the change by periodic reaffirmations.

Figure 6. Strategy Employment through the Stages of Change

Pre-contemplation

The pre-contemplation stage of readiness for change is where the client gives every reason why the discussed change is not or will not occur now because of a particular circumstance. As the coach, don't push the need for change or create a sense of guilt. After all, your role here is to continue to rehearse the positive aspects or benefits of an alternative behavior. Unfortunately, the client's sustain talk encourages a desire to keep the status quo and justifies the need to maintain the undesirable negative habits, which you can't change for that leader.

Contemplation

The contemplation stage still doesn't shift the client's mindset into a state of unequivocal decisive action toward the change. Here, the coach should encourage steps toward the desired goal and reflect back to the client any sustained talk while by permission, educating on any missing conceptual and behavioral gaps.

Preparation

When the client begins to prepare action steps and talk about change, lend support where needed and provide adequate coaching guidance, which confirms the need to continue preparing for action.

Action

At the action stage, your coaching prowess is most desirable as you identify gaps in the current action steps so that you can coach to the gaps. The action stage compels your expertise and requires patience to coach in areas that you identify as gaps in people, processes, and performance.

Maintenance

By the time you get to the client's maintenance stage, your role becomes more of an accountability partner to foster performance and sustain the desired behavior. At this stage, the leader is entirely responsible and aware of the impact of his or her efforts. The leader needs a strategy and accountability partner and not a cheerleader.

Termination

When the client is at this stage, you have done your job. You have effectively confirmed that the desired behavior modification is sustainable and that it will yield the measure of impact expected of the client to accomplish his or her wellness goals.

SUSTAINING COGNITIVELY CONNECTED LEADERSHIP BEHAVIOR

To stay cognitively connected, or in other words, to be fully aware of one's unconscious biases with the interrelationships among the physical, social, and mental and their impacts on one's behavior means that one can overcome any inherent leadership gaps. Bridging these leadership gaps to keep the leader cognitively connected takes adherence to a coaching schedule, which, over time, addresses both blind spot and open aspects of the Johari window (a concept that illustrates one's windows of social self-awareness) and one's stage in the trans theoretical change model. In essence, it examines the level of self-awareness and then the stage of readiness for change, when and where it is needed in the leader's sphere of influence. A firm grasp and confidence in these two paradigms enable the cognitively connected leader to remain effective at the basics of leadership and as a force multiplier in communicating visionary excellence when required. Such a leader understands inherent strengths and weaknesses and knows when to take action for desired outcomes.

To become fully functional in the present as a leader and continue to perform in the capacity of a transformed or healthy leader, one must master the following five tenets to sustain one's positive behavior, which leads to visionary excellence and enhanced cognitive awareness to govern behavior.

1. Introspection

Always have an introspective attitude toward leadership actions. As a leadership coach, you must communicate this imperative to your client. Self-reflection and intuitive perceptions must nurture an attitude of constant self-improvement. One cannot improve upon one's self-limiting behaviors until one comes to terms with acknowledging inherent fears and deciding to take positive steps toward overcoming them. When you discover these fears from the client, communicate your senses without imposing your sentiments or suggesting an action. Just strive to be present in the moment and assume you are wrong until proven right based on what your client says.

2. Positive Mental Attitude (PMA)

Napoleon Hill stated how essential a PMA is to overcome any setbacks in one's mind. This need cannot be overstated for a leader because a PMA is all one has available to fall back on when all else fails. During the coaching relationship and sessions, the need to stay positive at all times and consistently reflect on the positive aspects of any negative trends from the client may allow the leader to focus on what has worked or works to encourage behavior modification.

3. Healthy Social Relationships

Human interactions with positive people are imperative for healthy cognitive behavior among leaders. Leaders must depend on healthy social relationships so that they don't feel lonely at the top, as the saying goes. The caliber of relationships surrounding the leader is essential to their performance in any given environment. Therefore, the coach must coach and monitor the circle of influence. The leader client has to understand them better. Asking questions regarding the types and impacts of social influences of the leader creates an opportunity to self-examine whether any of those social relationships may be hindering or helping foster the desired behavioral change. The value and impact one's environment play in anyone's life should never be underestimated and never be overlooked if the client will modify his or her behavior.

4.   A Refined Physical and Mental (Spiritual) Balance

During the coaching relationship, it is essential to determine whether the leader's physical and mental habits have played a part in why the client expresses the current behavior. Physical health conditions the leader's body and tolerance for action and performance, but mental and spiritual health prepares and certifies the leader's readiness and confidence to modify behavior for change. The balance between one's physical and mental health rests on the strength of a support structure that nurtures a healthy balance. For instance, a leader who is physically out of shape and who seemingly looks morbidly obese will likely have a lower self-esteem and confidence level to stand before his or her team members to encourage them to take good care of themselves so that they are not burned out. Understanding the leader's perceived notions and impressions about self-esteem in relation to his or her physical health may be a critical component to knowing where that leader is if you want to begin or continue a coaching relationship focused on behavior modification. If the leader makes light of his or her physical appearance and if the leader is not cognitively disturbed, concerned, or motivated to improve, no amount of reference to physical health will alter his or her behavior. If your client is health-conscious, determined to make a move or an effort toward sound healthy living to improve his or her well-being, listening for change talk and a willingness to be coached are clear indicators of a transformational opportunity to modify behavior.

5.   A Clear Sense of Purpose (Vision)

When leaders have a clear sense of purpose, their organization is almost always healthy in all operations. So the leader leads well to create a harmonious, effective, and welcoming working environment. With a clear vision, leaders can identify the next milestones and steps required to get his or her desired organizational outcomes. Any unconscious behaviors that arise will almost always be curbed and shaped by the clarity of purpose and mind that the leader has. Therefore, having a well-informed and coached leader who has a clear view of the vision is like having a compass. No matter which way the wind blows into the sails of the mariner, the truth of the compass needle will always point the mariner back, just as the vision will to a clearly focused leader. When instinctive behavior occurs, having a direction and purpose to lead toward will almost certainly provide resolve from an unconscious behavior.

When a visionary wins, the visionary has attained a vision that was probably berthed several years before it came to fruition. A clear sense of purpose and clarity of mind makes this feasible.

CHAPTER 12

What It Takes to Resolve the Leadership Problem

Success requires persistence, the ability
to not give up in the face of failure.

—Martin Seligman
(American psychologist)

WHEN I WAS a young and freshly minted Ensign in the US Navy, I knew that I didn't know everything and that everything I didn't know was not only a result of ignorance regarding what it took to lead but also inexperience in the office I was to hold. Someone had to mentor me, someone had to lead me, and more importantly, someone had to coach me through the leadership flaws I had. No one had time for that, not even my commanding officer at the time, whose responsibility was to groom those under his leadership. Life as an ensign is about drinking from a fire hose and being a sponge ready to absorb everything you are required to learn over a short period to qualify in your profession and specialty. I quickly discovered a leadership gap in the way I was leading my division and the way I was being led. There was also a mentorship gap, which only mutual self-awareness by both the mentor and mentee could fix. The problem in this particular leadership environment was an absence of self-determination and self-awareness of cognitive shortcomings, which were framed by my past experiences of self-doubt and a fixed mindset. This was a leadership gap. Leaders and mentors whom I would depend on appeared to be self-absorbed in their own quest for self-validation and self-aggrandizement, to the extent that they missed several professional development gaps within the organization. While I was naive and inexperienced in my office as a leader, my supposed mentor or coach was caught up in a snare of being inward-focused instead of being outward-focused on growing a healthy, vibrant, and dynamic team. This perception of flawed organizational leadership was a cultural sentiment shared by others, so I knew my judgment wasn't egocentric—I needed coaching. Therefore, to solve such a leadership problem, no amount of book reading or motivational speeches would shift behavior to bridge the cognitive, transformational gap except a coaching process from someone who could appreciate my past, understand my present state and that of the leadership culture, and adequately coach me through a desired future of sound mental health and wellness. So the point is that resolving the leadership problem takes a holistic coaching approach with the individual leader by developing a mindset and mindful environment that elicits change for the desirable future while understanding the individual leader's desired professional goals.

What it takes to resolve the leadership problem is firstly, an acknowledgment that there is a problem that warrants resolution, which requires a change process. Secondly, it takes leaders willing to partner with someone who has intuitive expertise, such as a leadership health and wellness coach, and who is committed to a mutual goal of attaining success for his or her client. However, in situations where it is evident that a leadership gap exists, one of the single most important factors that needs addressing is the identification of who the leader is and what action steps or implementation strategies he or she has adapted already to remedy any blatantly obvious gaps that inhibit productivity and organizational performance. Knowing the history or baseline of attempted actions provides you, the leadership coach, an opportunity to understand where you are concerning the client's well-being or success path and where you want to go with that individual. *The Coaching Psychology Manual of 2016*[35] highlighted the four coaching mechanisms of action that must be present for an effective coaching process to attain its goals successfully. They are the following:

1. Building a coaching relationship that fosters brain learning and mindset growth
2. A client that is intrinsically motivated and holistically committed to change
3. A client that exudes utmost confidence that change is attainable and needful
4. A coach and client commitment to the coaching process of behavior modification tools and strategies

Overall, resolving the leadership problem does not happen overnight. It does not change amidst adversity, and it does not stop after overcoming one behavioral battle. It takes constant self-awareness and a growth mindset of health and wellness to perform at one's peak. Therefore, the leader must be fully aware of performance gaps and

---

[35]   Margaret Moore, Erika Jackson, and Bob Moran Tschaman, *Coaching Psychology Manual,* 2nd edition (Well Coaches Corporation, 2016) 12.

desirable actions to remedy them. The leader must be consciously active, compelling the coach to be equally attuned and connected to match the client's energy at a given time. The client leader must be consciously aware of who he or she is and what it will take to excel in his or her dysfunction. The leadership health and wellness coach must be equally conscious of the scope of the leadership problem if he or she is to be a change agent.

Consciousness, defined as awareness of self in space and time, means that you are as aware as the client is of the situation that requires coaching. Remember that there is a problem. Otherwise, your role as a coach would be a moot need. A problem needs a resolution, and you are an ideal candidate to do so because you have mastered the Triple C methodology and questioning technique well enough to bring the leader to resolve. You are bringing the leader through the past and into the present as that individual seeks his or her quest for significance and business or organizational success. To resolve the problem, you must nurture a culture of self-awareness with the client through the coaching relationship and leave the client with a sense of responsibility and accountability for success. To do so takes practice, confidence, connectedness, consistency, foresight, and the discipline of execution for the organizational leader.

Clearly, there are several challenges that one might face as a leader. They may not solely be attributed to one's past inhibitions, unconscious impulsive behaviors, or strange mannerisms that may constitute a problem. Frankly, there may be no problem with his or her leadership skills or decision-making at any level. There may be a very sound balance among the leader's physical, social, and mental health states. However, a problem may lie in the leader's ability to adjust to the environment in which that person finds himself or herself. It's about culture and team dynamics. It's about being physically, socially, and mentally healthy enough to adapt to a world in flux. These factors influence the outcomes of organizational well-being. The way the leader thrives or perceives success in these contexts can dramatically affect how successful the leader becomes. In his book *Good to Great: Why Some Companies Make the Leap and Others Don't*, author Jim Collins mentions the need for a disciplined culture. He notes that bureaucracy exists to mitigate the effects of a lack of discipline, which stems from "a problem that largely goes away if you have the right people."[36] So you see, it sometimes boils down to people in the wrong places creating unwanted or needless bottlenecks, which could have been easily avoided if people were in their right frames of mind or adequately coached through challenging aspects of the organizational well-being.

To resolve any problem, one must be prepared to commit to resolving what lies at the core of the problem and not just address the symptoms. Remember that one has to be coached through the cognitive stages, from the unconscious to the preconscious and through to one's conscious actions. Does a good leader need to be coached through how to cope with his or her environment or team of people due to a difference in culture? Likely! Does the leader understand a need to do so and therefore, solicit the services of a leadership health and wellness coach? I certainly hope so. So what it takes to resolve the leadership problem is simple: a committed coaching relationship between a leader who is smart enough to know that he or she doesn't have all the answers but is willing to clear the blind spots. That person is a certified leadership health and wellness coach who understands the connected cognitive process and the leader client well enough to commit all their Triple C expertise and resources to help that leader excel in their sphere of influence.

When the two can build an effective and trustworthy rapport, all the pieces for resolution and the gaps to be bridged begin to fall in place. There is enough work to resolve stressful moments in a

---

[36]   Jim Collins, *Good to Great: Why Some Companies Make the Leap and Others Don't* (New York, NY: Harper Collins Publishers, 2001) 120.

leader's personal or professional life. There is much opportunity to change an organization's conduct, concerns, and culture if the leader or leaders commit to teaching a vibrant learning mindset among team members or followers. The leadership problem has never been about the absence of competent organizational leaders. It has most often been about the systemic presence of a lackadaisical attitude toward positional leadership. In this leadership, most take for granted the assumption that stressed and mentally drained leaders in positions are the solution and that the status quo in leadership is acceptable. Unfortunately, this paradigm of impoverished leadership prevails no matter how unhealthy it may be among leaders who are not cognitively well. Most people caught in the paradigm of that's just the way he is or that's just how she's wired allow these notions to permeate organizations, which leads to mediocrity and substandard performance across organizations. Though these personality dispositions may be true, they are neither acceptable nor sustainable for an organization's performance. Soon, the organization must come to its knees apologetically for failing its members and corrupting its essence with poor, adulterated, and dysfunctional leadership. A leader or leaders who don't know better will fail because they have either not been taught better or have failed to allow themselves enough room to grow in an environment that challenges their worth and questions their mettle. Any leader who fails to create an environment for performance feedback is destined for self and organizational implosion because one will always have a blind spot that warrants another's perspective to stay on course with the mission at hand. This is where the leadership health and wellness coach comes in. The coach partners with leaders to make an impact in helping the challenged leader get healthy and well. How can the leadership health and wellness coach help the client understand concerns or leadership gaps? Start with recognizing and acknowledging that there is a problem at hand.

PROBLEM ACKNOWLEDGEMENT FOR RESOLUTION

Often when there is a problem, a leader who wears a type A personality proudly will hardly admit that he or she has a leadership problem. In many cases, the leader is likely to see any problem as a poor systematic or process flaw that has nothing to do with his or her ability to lead. The leader might even find ways to remove others in office if there appears to be a shred of resistance to the way things should be for the leader's whims and caprices to thrive. Change may hardly come or may not come easily for one stuck in this situation. A few years ago, I was on a leadership team with a man who was so self-consumed with his arrogance and pride that he never admitted to any of his actions as a potential fault. He often argued his way out of important decisions we had to make if they required his sound judgment. Over time, this state of cognitive inhibition affected members of his team. I understood his challenge, but I couldn't help someone unwilling to see that he could potentially be at risk of losing his official position as a leader in the organization. Over time, he lost his marriage and his position in the organization. You see, he was sure that everyone was wrong, and he was always right despite several attempts by others to remind him of specific detrimental actions. He was in a state of denial that he needed to change his behavior. In this case, a leader stuck at the pre-contemplation stage will have little value for your service or help until he or she encounters a brick wall of encumbrances and overwhelming challenges. However, subtle indicators for change should always be a welcomed effort for a leader who just lacks self-awareness but wants collective change for the well-being of the organization. One of the most painful experiences I had was watching a leader who was so self-absorbed in his ego that he dismissed the manager from a meeting because the manager was ahead of him in her knowledge and delivery of required reports. She was on top of her game, which made the leader look bad. At least, that was the perception created. If this was not a case of a cognitively unhealthy leader, I don't know how to describe it. The fact is, as a young leader, I found it confusing why a leader would not want team members or subordinates to know more than the leader did if they were experts in their roles. Why wouldn't the leader want them to stay ahead of him or her to ensure that they are supporting every effort to accomplish the collective mission? When leaders think or believe that it is all about them, they stifle the progress of the team and create a vacuum where only they can suck the air out of the room to feed their egos. This behavior and lack of self-awareness is an unhealthy environment, which leadership health and wellness coaches must seek to help leaders resolve.

During the war in Iraq, a platoon leader in charge of a team of marines was on a mission with a convoy of troops when one vehicle was hit by an improvised explosive device, rendering it immobile. Quickly, everyone knew what to do as they followed his directions and positioned themselves. They were ready to fulfill the mission despite the setback they had just encountered. They had a problem that needed to be solved. At the moment of the impact, he was ready for such an occurrence, so he quickly signaled his team members to take cover while he checked each member's status by radio. He communicated the status of affairs to higher headquarters. He recalled that at the time of the attack, he had three things on his mind: his team members' safety, the mission's impact, and how to neutralize any prevailing threats that might follow due to a possible ambush. His mind had to be in the right place at the right time. He had to be with the right people, who would act upon his orders and accomplish the mission. However, if at any point leading up to this incident, he had been verbally abusive, irresponsible, or negligent (the core of the problem to be acknowledged) with any of his team members in any undue manner, his orders would have been undermined and compromised in a life-and-death situation. This vulnerability would have been because of previous experiences or encounters that suggested a less-than-optimal working relationship with his team members. Someone would have challenged his arrogance, which could have led to mutiny, if trusting him was questionable. The point is that he had earned his team members' trust, confidence, and respect well before problems had to be solved in this austere environment. This healthy relationship with team members must have occurred by the way he treated them and carried himself so that when there was a problem, everyone rallied around the leader, solved it, and celebrated after a collective victory. Where there is dysfunction and distrust because the leader's conduct is unhealthy, the organization's mission and team are at risk, and ultimately, the whole team loses. Success in resolving a problem starts with the leader's command of the team. If his authority, trust, and conduct are undermined, the entire organization is vulnerable to failure. Success in problem-solving starts with the leader.

COACHING RELATIONSHIP

The leadership health and wellness coach is uniquely responsible for listening to the client and ensuring the adequate attainment of the client's goals and wellness vision. Remember that the coach is the transformational vehicle of change for the client, but the responsibility of a healthy coaching relationship also rests with the client. If the client wants help or expertise, he or she will tune in to the wellness process and allow coaching to occur. However, suppose either party feels that there is a challenge in building the required rapport to move on. Then it is the coach's responsibility to terminate the coaching relationship under regulated ethical stipulations. The coaching relationship predicates an environment where the coach is mindful of the client's state of mind at the time and place of the meeting. The dialogue is authentic, with open-ended inquiries that elicit positive reflections of thought. When a coach can adequately match the client's energy level, he or she can build a rapport each time for coaching to occur. As the leadership health and wellness coach, your mandate is to create this safe and cordial environment, which is unencumbered by distractions or self-serving agendas. It is always about the client's desires and never about what you want for the client. If the client wants success, you naturally do. Otherwise, neither can nurture a relationship, and coaching certainly doesn't occur.

In a coaching relationship, you cannot overstate the coach's responsibility to create a safe and welcoming environment. For the relationship to be well-nurtured, the client must feel his or her needs are met over time and after establishing the initial rapport. The leader's physical, mental, and social gaps or challenges must be quickly identified in the first few sessions when establishing the wellness vision and goals. A successful relationship that ultimately solves the leadership problem almost always starts with understanding the client's cognitive health at any point in his or her life. If the client feels there is no problem to solve, the coach can do little as the client stays in the pre-contemplation stage of behavior. However, it is incumbent upon the coach to probe actions and question intents to help the client become self-aware of his or her leadership gap. What is at the core of the mental, physical, or social inhibition that the client expresses? As the coach, you must ultimately make it your mission to help your client overcome his or her cognitive block. Three things to consider as you attempt to bridge this gap and overcome the cognitive block, time, place, and opportunity are these:

Time: Is it the right time to elicit or probe the gap for the client's sustained action?
Place: Is the setting or environment conducive to addressing the identified gap?

Opportunity: Can the issue be introduced due to an ideal timing
   situation?

When you identify the right time for the client to take action
regarding his or her concerns, you also consider whether the client
will be able to sustain it in the given environment over the course
of the time required for behavior modification. If both (time and
place) are ripe, seek an opportunity to remind the client why he or
she desires that change—why not now? Often, because the cognitive
block lingers and makes it hard to break through to the client, a negative impact on any one of the three factors jeopardizes the success
of the coaching relationship. However, you should break through
to bring resolve because you are well-connected in your intuitive
approach. Bad timing may yield failure if there is insufficient time to
get healthy. The wrong environment for change may exacerbate the
health and wellness of your client due to negative influences. You are
farther from accomplishing the mission if the opportunity to elicit
action or probing dialogue doesn't occur. Therefore, be sensitive to
the right or ideal time, place, and opportunity to strike a healthy
coaching dialogue when the iron is hot.

A SUCCESSFUL OUTCOME

For a successful outcome, the client must be unapologetically and
blatantly honest about concerns, feelings, the desired end state, and
expected future outcomes from the coaching relationship, considering how actions impact those led. It takes a good team and a good
leader to be a successful organization. This sense of awareness is
imperative for a healthy leader to attain if he or she wants a level
measure of effectiveness. However, a well-designed outcome must
be at the forefront of the leader's mind to get there. The 5-D cycle
of appreciative inquiry, which was initially propounded by David

Cooperrider and adopted in *The Coaching Psychology Manual,* suggests that teams and organizations can achieve their best outcomes if they intentionally do so by defining, discovering, dreaming, designing, and being destined for success[37]. A leader who bears the responsibility of creating a productive and peaceful professional environment will *define* his or her objectives, will *discover* what inspires or what gaps exist that need to be bridged. They will *dream* as big as the mind allows, will *design* what kind of outcome the client desires to see, and then ultimately, will allow the leader to be coached through attaining his or her *destiny*. Leaders often excel and do well when they have set clear goals and when they are accountable to someone to be successful. It is a mutual responsibility to attain the client's stated goals.

Coaching is the easier part of attaining the results the client desires. The harder part is getting a leader to identify a blatantly obvious problem. Maybe it is a fear deeply rooted in the subconscious mind or a fact of knowledge that shapes the feared situation in the preconscious mind. The leader can confidently and boldly modify behavior by acting on his or her compulsions through the conscious mind. Whatever the circumstance, a successful outcome takes teamwork to get there. The true legacy of success is the impact of transformational influence in the lives of leaders who live to tell across generations the extent of your influence long after you are gone. John Maxwell's book *The Leader's Greatest Return: Attracting, Developing, and Multiplying Leaders* reminds me of a favorite quote from Phil Jackson: "The strength of the pack is the wolf, and the strength of the wolf is the pack."[38] This quote is such a profound statement, which illustrates the essence of the whole team in making

---

[37]   Margaret Moore, Erika Jackson, and Bob Tschaman-Moran, *The Coaching Psychology Manual* (2nd ed.) (Well Coaches Corporation, 2016) 68.

[38]   John Maxwell, *The Leader's Greatest Return: Attracting, Developing, and Multiplying Leaders* (Harper Collins Leadership, 2020) 143. Chapter quotes retrieved from *www.azquotes.com.*

one powerful attribute. Without that powerful attribute one has as a leader, the team loses its strength. In the same light, the leadership health and wellness coach and the client are a team. They are a team that partners to attain a united goal in a concerted effort. Remember, the client is always in the driver's seat of his or her leadership health and wellness. The coach is only sitting shotgun. This teamwork must be carefully and adequately nurtured to achieve the client's desired results so that the leader with an unhealthy foundation or past can gradually and systematically work through any inhibitions. Consequently, finding ways to develop, nurture, and ultimately, make one leader healthy and well will compel the leader to be consciously aware of his or her strengths and challenges so that the leader can excel in sound decision-making.

CONCLUSION

Leadership health and wellness coaches will be recognized in small business sectors, educational institutions, medical facilities, and ecclesiastical organizations as agents of transformational change for leaders who are challenged by stressful moments and troubled pasts. This book serves as a foundation upon which the Leadership Health and Wellness book series builds to address coaching mechanics and approaches for stress management while seeking to improve leaders' physical, social, and mental well-being in those sectors. The seat of professional excellence and brilliance in cognitive performance rests with those who take time to seek self-improvement every day. They never assume they have all the answers to the tests of life. They seek ways to enhance or mend the power of their minds.

The power of the mind to heal itself depends on the strength of the environment in which it feeds. When leaders can accept the connection between the states of consciousness and the impacts on their leadership prowess, they will begin to function at their peak performances. Yet if the mind knows only fear because it is consistently and conclusively bathed in hostility and deprived of the freedom of free thought, it will become seared by impending doom and never be at peace to lead. This condition is unhealthy. It breeds a negative response to the social environment, which cannot transform positivity and wellness across all spectra of the social class. It breeds a hostile working environment cultivated by a troubled leader. The leader who is hurt hurts followers. A leader who is unhealthy will progressively become worse if not medicated by sound counsel, self-reflection, or positive cognitive influence. Therefore, what the Triple C methodology hopes to accomplish through effective employment across coaching relationships is an opportunity to heal through time, patience, and mindful presence with a connection by a certified leadership health and wellness coach.

This well-trained and empathetic professional understands the need to bring an unhealthy leader from a state of self-denial to a place of self-awareness so that the leader can attain the highest level of professional excellence. This excellence will occur if the client leader is truthfully sincere and coachable. This transformation will occur over time if the coaching environment remains sound and safe. This attainment of essence and peace can be realized when clients give coaching a chance and when coaches offer mindfulness at all times. I hope to see the value of leadership health and wellness coaching as a staple in professional organizations, institutions of higher learning, and more importantly, evidence of its results in a well-coached leader who has endured the patience of humility and the courage of marred professionalism toward an opportunity for hope and into a transformed leader and organization. The figure below illustrates the path to attaining the desired outcome of a leader from a state of ambivalence and absence of cognitive clarity evident in their subconscious mind, to a state of full well-being expressed through the conscious mind in their sound mental/spiritual, physical and social health. Consequently, a healthy leader will be faith-full, relational, de-stressed, impressive, influential, energetic, and well-balanced in their leadership performance to make sound decisions.

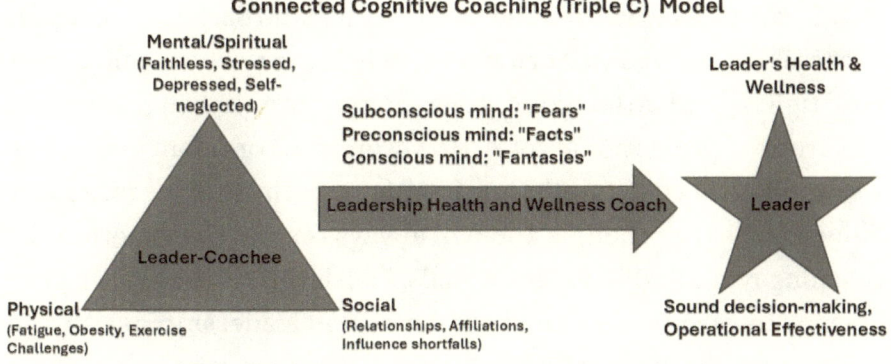

Figure 7. The Leader's Wellness Path

Tomorrow, the sun might set on those who never dared to allow themselves an opportunity to change. Yet today remains the only sure moment of self-awareness and introspection that reveals who we truly are within and what we truly want to become to the world. If, and only if, we are willing to be vulnerably ready to change our minds when and where needed for healthy leadership and a well-balanced social, physical, and mental states, we will realize the power of exceptional leadership, which transforms leadership that only a healthy mind and sound body can foster. So as you coach or lead, consider the tenets in this book and the intents they convey. Practice the strategies and encourage the desired outcomes so that when coaching is all said and done, whether in a small-business service organization, a health-care setting, or an educational institution, there will be no doubt that a once unhealthy leader has been transformed through a process that seeks to uncover deeply rooted truths to help overcome unsolicited actions and move toward a healthy and professional lifestyle.

As the world of professional coaching continues to grow, leaders will need an ally who will be their wingman or woman to overcome challenging feats in business, health care, or education. You will need a resource: *Leadership Health and Wellness for Small Business Leaders* or *Leadership Health and Wellness for Healthcare Leaders*. These resources should provide clear and tailored coaching approaches. As coaches in these sectors, you will bring resolve to leaders who would otherwise fight their battles alone while they endure challenges across a spectrum of professional roles. However, I am confident you will be well-poised to coach well. Coach with empathy and mindfulness, knowing that the client is and will always remain the expert in the coaching relationship to attain goals. I wish you all the best on your journey toward being a renowned certified leadership health and wellness coach who is confidently proud and eagerly optimistic about the transformational change that awaits anyone with whom you have the unique pleasure and opportunity to work with in realizing his or her desired outcomes!

Stay blessed and continue to *lead the change!*